Selected Poems of Carl Sandburg

Selected Poems
of Carl Sandburg

Edited by

Rebecca West

New York

Harcourt, Brace and Company

PRINTED IN THE U. S. A. BY
QUINN & BODEN COMPANY, INC.
RAHWAY, N. J.

Contents

From **CHICAGO POEMS**

Contents

From CORNHUSKERS

Contents

Contents

Contents

Contents

From *SLABS OF THE SUNBURNT WEST*

Contents

Preface

THERE is in America an incredible city named Chicago: a rain-coloured city of topless marble towers that stand among waste plots knee-high with tawny grasses beside a lake that has grey waves like the sea. It has a shopping and office district that for miles round is a darkness laid on the eyes, so high are the buildings, so cluttered up are the narrow streets with a gauntly striding elevated railway, and a stockyards district that for miles round is a stench in the nostrils. It has rows of rotting, paintless timber houses, each with a veranda, each with a rocking-chair on its veranda, most with a scoured rag drying on the chipped balustrade of that veranda, which go on mile after mile and end at long length in marshes where wild birds circle round the dark keeps of breweries abandoned because of a certain vast and catastrophic legislative gesture. It has vast stretches of flat suburbs which, though they are the homes of the comfortable, have a nightmare quality, for one may travel northward ten, fifteen, twenty miles and apparently pass and repass the same fifty yards, since there is nothing on either side save the same villa standing at exactly the same distance from its identical fellows in the same featureless, hedgeless gardens on straight roads of exactly the same width, except where there is some such unpredictable variation as a vast temple raised to the nineteenth-century Persian prophet known as the Bab. Extravagant weather passes over this extravagant city. In the summer you may sit in the dining-room of a magnificent hotel built like an Italian palazzo and look down on the waters of the lake which no longer seem water, because they are packed with people from the slums who have run into the lake because they are sweating, scorching, blistering with the unbearable heat of the Middle West until they have no room to swim but must stand upright, crowded shoulder to shoulder. The older of them cry through the twilight in tongues you have not heard since you were last in Budapest or Athens or Prague, and the younger in a tongue that you will not understand if you come from England, though it is English. In winter, even so late as April, you may walk for an hour by that same lake and not meet a soul, so bitter is the wind that blows over the ice-bank that lips its edge.

Though Chicago sprawls widely across Illinois, it has but a third of the population of London. It has, however, an Opera such as London has not. It has an Art Gallery which alone would make the journey to these parts worth while, particularly for those who care about modern French art. It has an important book-buying public which wrangles over modern literature for fear the road to the truth should be closed like Englishmen disputing over rights of way. It experiments passionately with every new method of social technique, affixing, for example, a psychological clinic to their law courts in which theory after theory is tried out in feverish haste so that at one time it seems to be proved that all criminals in Chicago are without exception the victims of *dementia præcox* and at another that they are all epileptics. Everybody has their fun. The poor dance wildly in dance-halls the size of cathedrals, they have their movie theatres vast as the Pantheon and naïve as a small boy, and they have a real endowment in an ardent civic consciousness such as is not now known in the Old World. Every child in the street will tell you how beautiful Michigan Boulevard will be when it is finished, and looks forward, as to a consummation of personal self-satisfaction, to the day, which in point of fact is inevitably approaching, when Chicago will be the capital of the United States.

But also Chicago has crime such as London has not. There is, roughly speaking, a murder a day. This crime occasionally takes spectacular and portentous forms. Only a few years ago, following a dispute between whites and negroes at a bathing-shore, Chicago took a holiday from its business for five days and carried on a race-riot, killing over thirty people, wounding over five hundred, and destroying a thousand homes. Another racial problem had as sinister a crystallization there in a recent murder. A rich Jewish boy was so impressed as a child by the hatred and contempt directed by Christians at his race (for Anti-Semitism in the United States is a savage thing) that, when his father took him for company in his car to the office in the mornings by a route which passed the penitentiary recreation ground, he identified himself and his kind with the convicts. In the course of time, because of this early identification, his natural desire to excel among his own people confusedly expressed itself as a desire to

17

excel among criminals; so that with the help of another Jew, who was an easy victim to him since he also had been warped by a fantasy arising out of a sense of racial persecution, he committed a senseless murder. It is worth while paying attention to the vehement and significant character of these crimes, because this is simply one aspect of a general vehemence and significance of life in this region.

These peculiarities spring from a certain peculiarity of the individual lives of its inhabitants. The normal citizen there is living a very intense life of self-consciousness and self-analysis. The external manifestation of this is a curious loquacity which is at once more personal and more impersonal than any corresponding talkativeness one might encounter in Europe. People who sit opposite one in a dining-car, or who wait on one as manicurists or shop-assistants or hotel servants, are ready to tell one the story of their lives without the smallest provocation, and to round it off by attempts to derive from it some helpful cosmic principle. It is as likely as not that a taxi-driver, when one pays one's fare, will not consider the transaction closed. He may pause to ask if one is French, and on receiving the answer that one is not, will express surprise on the ground that one is dark and he was under the impression that all English people are fair; he will impart to one the domestic circumstances which prevented him from going to France with the American Expeditionary Force; and he will say that he regrets it, for he loves to move about the world, and is indeed at this moment thinking of going to Kansas City and working there for a bit; and he will end by wondering why man loves to wander, and what it profits him, since in essentials life is the same everywhere. He will tell his story slowly, and he will seem to expect one to stand by when he tells it; and indeed, though the Americans are the most speedy people in the world, so far as dealing with mechanical devices, in making or driving an automobile, or in organizing and operating a telephone system, they are infinitely leisurely when it is a matter of giving or receiving self-explanations.

It occurs to one, as such experiences accumulate, that one has encountered in art, though not in life, people who talk and behave like this: in Russian novels. There one gets precisely the same universal addiction to self-consciousness and self-analysis. And then it occurs to one also that this place is in certain respects very like Russia. Chicago, like Leningrad, like Moscow, is a high spot, to use its own idiom, on the monotony of great plains; a catchment area of vitality that rejoices extravagantly in its preservation because elsewhere in this region it might have trickled away from its source and been swallowed up in the vastness of the earth. All round Chicago lies the Middle Western plain. It stretches in every direction, a day's journey to the east, a day and a night and a day to the west, and more than that to the south: flat, oozy, the longest possible span from horizon to horizon. All the fields look the same whether one looks from the train just after dawn or before nightfall on any of these journeys; and again and again one passes the same village, for here man has had so much to do in merely covering the ground that he has neither time nor energy to develop variations of his establishment. What with the clouds and the moon and the stars, it often seems as if there is more doing in the sky than on earth. The physical resemblance between Russia and the Middle West is certainly close enough. And it may be that life which finds itself lost in the heart of a vast continent, whether that be Old or New, has a tendency to take the same forms. Life in another case, which flows in a number of channels and is divided into small nations, is psychologically in a far more fortunate position. When it expresses itself it has all the neighbouring nations as an audience, who will give it a verdict on its performance, which is none the less useful if its inevitable function is to be disbelieved; and it has a basis for optimism about the universe, since it sees the neighbouring nations surviving and flourishing in spite of what it is bound to consider their inferiorities. But a nation that is isolated in its vastness has no audience but itself, and it has no guarantee that continued existence is possible or worth while, save its own findings. Therefore, Russia and Middle West alike, it is committed to introspection, to a constant stocktaking of its own life and a constant search for the meaning of it.

This entails various consequences. It accounts for the general quality of vehemence and significance which is common to both peoples. For a man who is self-conscious will emphasize his actions so that his self can the better

Preface

come to a conclusion regarding them, and since he is desirous that his self shall be able to draw some meaning from them he will be careful to put much meaning into them. It has other more particular results. It profoundly affects the language. All over the United States the stranger will note that the English and American languages are essentially different in genius in spite of their partial identity of vocabulary. But in the Middle West more than anywhere else the introspective inhabitants have developed an idiom which is exactly the reverse of our English tongue in that it is admirably suited for describing the events of the inner life and entirely inadequate in dealing with the events of the outer life. If one goes into an English police court one is safe to see a policeman go into the witness-box and say, 'At 11.30 p.m. on the night of Friday the 31st of July I was proceeding in the course of my duties down Bow Street,' as a prelude to a complete and comprehensible story of the physical events which happened in a certain point of space at a certain point of time. But he will not be able to give any impression at all of the psychological state of any of the personalities involved. This is not because he is a policeman. It is because he is speaking English. The learned counsel who undertook the defence of Mrs. Thompson in the Thompson and Bywaters case was utterly unable to convey to the jury any picture of the psychological state of his client. Now in the Chicago courts the case is far otherwise. On points of fact the police give evidence in a way that in this country would be thought phenomenally deplorable in the worst witness in an Assize court in a backward district. But they will give the most subtle and exact evidence about the psychological situation in each case. They may not even know the correct name of the crime of which they are accusing their prisoner, and have to use a slang phrase for it, but they will have on their tongues' ends beautiful and expressive phrases to describe the character of the house in which they found him, his bearing when they arrested him, and the reactions of the other persons concerned, phrases in which brilliantly chosen words have their meaning expanded by the cunningest use of rhythm. For the inhabitants of the Middle West, although to our European standards tone-deaf, are masters of rhythm. 'Getting by with it. . . .' It is the drawled rhythm which gives that phrase its tremendous irony, which makes it impossible to carry over all its contents into English-English, just as, they say, it is impossible to translate innumerable Russian words expressive of psychological states and processes.

Though introspection forges a beautiful instrument of expression, it sometimes provides matters which it is regrettable should be expressed. Sometimes through reflecting overmuch on the difficulties of life it becomes panic-stricken and tries to short-circuit them. Then it stumbles on the brilliant idea that existence would be much simpler if there were only one sort of people on earth, which is perfectly true. It broods on this idea until it magnifies it to falsity and comes to believe that all its troubles will be over if it destroys so far as possible all persons within its territories who are of a different kind

Preface

from the majority. In Russia this leads to Pogroms; and in the Middle West to Anti-Semitism, prejudice against the alien immigrants, and Anti-Negro race-riots. These are offences against justice and mercy, and injurious to the common conception of law. Therefore those who truly love their country swing the balance to the other side so far as they may by cultivating a comprehensive love for all human souls that find themselves within these territories and rejecting none from their fellowship: a love which though it is a pacifist and reconciling force has yet the fierceness of a movement in opposition.

Race-antagonism is not the only spiritual ill which springs from this alliance of introspection and isolation. There comes also a facile mysticism which satisfies too easily the instincts of religion and patriotism. Russia calls itself Holy Russia, which is the kind of name which had better be left for other people to apply; and the Middle West's insistence on its own idealism is often open to the same objection. In each case the mysticism amounts to a glorification of the *status quo* as the one road to spiritual perfection. In Russia the *status quo* is, for the mass of the inhabitants, poverty and suffering; therefore it is held that he who is bruised and starving is nearest to salvation. In America the *status quo* is, for the mass of the inhabitants, prosperity; therefore it is held that the go-getter is nearest to salvation. To the unprejudiced the one is not actually more unpleasing than the other. One has only to read one of the more mechanical practitioners of Russian mysticism, such as Mr. Stephen Graham, to realize that the simple Moujik is only Babbitt down on his luck. The offence of the one, which is the attempt to seek union with God through adherence to a formula, is equally the offence of the other. But this also, like race-antagonism, provokes a beautiful counter-movement among those who truly love their country. Such in Russia worked for a revolution which would raise the people out of their suffering and bring the whole world nearer to God by making life more harmonious. And such in the Middle West practise a withdrawal from the ways of prosperity, take flight into solitude and simple living, not as a panacea, but to get free from mob-suggestion and seek an individual relationship with God.

I have not yet mentioned Carl Sandburg, but I have been writing of him all the time. For he is the voice of this region. He is, like Robert Burns, a national poet. Just as Robert Burns expresses the whole life of Lowland Scotland of his time, so Carl Sandburg expresses the whole life of the Middle West of to-day. He has learned his country by heart. He was born of Swedish parentage in Galesburg, Illinois, in 1878. At the age of thirteen he left school and began driving a milk wagon. He subsequently became a bricklayer and a farm labourer on the wheat-growing plains of Kansas. After an interval spent in graduating in an Illinois University, he became an hotel servant in Denver, a coalheaver in Omaha, and a soldier in the Spanish-American war, and after that a journalist. He has published four books of poems, *Chicago Poems* (1915), *Cornhuskers* (1918), *Smoke and Steel* (1920), and *Slabs of the Sun-*

Preface

burnt West (1922). The qualities of the Middle West
are his qualities. The main determinant of his art is the
power of his native idiom to deal with the inner life of
man. He can describe the inner life, the not too bad
life, that lies behind the shapeless skyscrapers, like so
many giant petrol-cans, and the dreary timber houses
of an ordinary Middle Western town. He can describe
the inner life of the eager little girls who leave those
small towns and come to Chicago, but still find no world
that makes use of their sweetness. He can describe the
inner life of the strong young men who wander about
the vast land, proud and yet perplexed; proud because
they are lending their strength to the purposes of the
new civilization, perplexed because they do not know
what it is all about. His idiom shapes him also in mak-
ing him not so wise in his pictures of the external life.
In making this selection I have omitted nearly all his
objective nature poems because they strike the English
reader as intolerably loose statements of fact. Our
poets, whether Wordsworth writing about the Lakes, or
Edith Sitwell writing about a home-park, give you the
colour and texture and substance of the rocks, the waters,
the grass, and the trees they write of, as well as the lie
of their imagined country. That tendency in English
poetry is due probably to the keen eye of the farmer
intent on his crops, the squire intent on his hunting, and
the parson intent on his garden; and the knowing small
talk of one or other of these types has sounded in the
infant ears of most of our poets. We are therefore apt
to be shocked at Carl Sandburg when he dilutes his de-

scriptions of nature with abstract nouns and references to dreams in the manner of Mr. F. E. Weatherley. But his subjective nature poems, such as 'Prairie' and 'Potato Blossom Songs and Jigs', which describe the effects of the seasons as they sweep over these wide lands on the noticing kind of men there are thereabouts, are very beautiful.

That last poem is a brilliant example of Carl Sandburg's technical virtuosity. For he is characteristically Middle Western in that his poems have no great sense of melody but a strong sense of rhythm. It will be said of him by Philistines that his poetry has no music in it, particularly by such Philistines as do not, like the lady in the limerick, know 'God Save the Weasel' from 'Pop Goes the Queen.' The same sort of people accuse Cézanne, who was born with a mahl-stick in his hand, of painting as he did because he was incapable of painting like Leader. In point of fact, Carl Sandburg is an accomplished musician, who is famous both for his singing and for his researches into American folk-song, and the music of his poetry is based on the technique of the banjo, very much as Manuel de Falla's music is based on the technique of the guitar. It must be remembered that his lines will not reveal their music, and indeed have none to reveal, unless they are read with a Middle Western accent; which incidentally—and this is important because it gives time for the variations of rhythm to disclose themselves—is very much slower than English speech.

There is also in Carl Sandburg a full expression of

the counter-movements of those who truly love the
Middle West against those who love it not so well.
This might seem a consideration too purely moral and
political to be relevant to one's estimate of a poet; but
actually each of these counter-movements implies an
æsthetic liberation. It has been the tendency of
America to limit its art to the delineation of what is
called the Anglo-Saxon element within its territories.
This has been to deny the artist the right to use some of
the most entrancing brightly-coloured patterns that he
saw in the real world before him. Carl Sandburg uses
everything he sees that looks to him a good subject: Mrs.
Pietro Giovannitti, the Singing Nigger, the workmen
who 'spill Peloponnesian syllables' as they sit in a Chi-
cago lunch-room, the Hungarians with their kegs of
beer on the picnic green. And he writes of the navvy
and the hoodlum, not from any 'open road' infantilism,
but because they are at any rate men who withdraw
themselves from the areas of standardized living and
thinking and who can look at reality with their own eyes.
It must be remembered that in the United States, where
the big employers take enormous pains to shape the minds
of their workmen by welfare work, by the placarding of
the factories with impressive ukases, by the control of
the local press, and by the government of the towns they
build for their employees, a man who takes a well-paid
job is very often putting himself in a position where he
will find it difficult not to sign away his soul, or at least
his intellect. It is true that Carl Sandburg has kept
clear of that conspiracy largely because of a revolution-

Preface

ary passion that does both good and bad service to his talent. It sometimes inspires him to brilliant and delicate political writing. It is a curious fact that no writer of Anglo-Saxon descent, no representative of the New England tradition, has described the break between Lincoln's America and modern industrialized America so poignantly as Carl Sandburg has. But his revolutionary passion so often betrays him, for poem after poem is ruined by a coarsely intruding line that turns it from poetry to propaganda. But the effect of this resistance to his environment is in sum an æsthetic benefit. It enables him to write of the real America, which one might describe to the present-day, over-prosperous America, in the words of one of its own advertisements, as 'the Venus beneath your fat'. In 'Prairie' and 'The Windy City' and 'Slabs of the Sunburnt West', he has evoked the essential America which will survive when this phase of commercial expansion is past and the New World is cut down to the quick as the Old World is to-day: a vast continent which by the majesty of its plains and its waters and its mountains, calls forth a response of power in the men who behold it, now that they are white as it did when they were red. His is not a talent that is too easily accepted in this age, which is inclined to regard poetry as necessarily lyric and to demand that the poet shall write brief and perfect verse; but the reason he cannot satisfy such standards is that his art is dominated by an image so vast that it requires as house-room not one but a thousand poems.

REBECCA WEST.

28

1.   Chicago

HOG Butcher for the World,
   Tool Maker, Stacker of Wheat,
   Player with Railroads and the Nation's Freight
      Handler;
   Stormy, husky, brawling,
   City of the Big Shoulders:

They tell me you are wicked, and I believe them; for I
   have seen your painted women under the gas lamps
   luring the farm boys.
And they tell me you are crooked, and I answer: Yes, it
   is true I have seen the gunman kill and go free to
   kill again.
And they tell me you are brutal, and my reply is: On
   the faces of women and children I have seen the
   marks of wanton hunger.
And having answered so I turn once more to those who
   sneer at this my city, and I give them back the
   sneer and say to them:
Come and show me another city with lifted head singing
   so proud to be alive and coarse and strong and
   cunning.
Flinging magnetic curses amid the toil of piling job on
   job, here is a tall bold slugger set vivid against the
   little soft cities;
Fierce as a dog with tongue lapping for action, cunning
   as a savage pitted against the wilderness,

Chicago

        Bareheaded,
        Shovelling,
        Wrecking,
        Planning,
        Building, breaking, rebuilding,
Under the smoke, dust all over his mouth, laughing with
        white teeth,
Under the terrible burden of destiny laughing as a young
        man laughs,
Laughing even as an ignorant fighter laughs who has
        never lost a battle,
Bragging and laughing that under his wrist is the pulse,
        and under his ribs the heart of the people,
                        Laughing!
Laughing the stormy, husky, brawling laughter of
        Youth, half-naked, sweating, proud to be Hog
        Butcher, Tool Maker, Stacker of Wheat, Player
        with Railroads and Freight Handler to the Nation.

2. Lost

DESOLATE and lone
All night long on the lake
Where fog trails and mist creeps,
The whistle of a boat
Calls and cries unendingly,
Like some lost child
In tears and trouble
Hunting the harbour's breast
And the harbour's eyes.

3. The Harbour

PASSING through huddled and ugly walls
  By doorways where women
    Looked from their hunger-deep eyes,
    Haunted with shadows of hunger-hands,
    Out from the huddled and ugly walls,
    I came sudden, at the city's edge,
    On a blue burst of lake,
    Long lake waves breaking under the sun
    On a spray-flung curve of shore;
    And a fluttering storm of gulls,
    Masses of great grey wings
    And flying white bellies
    Veering and wheeling free in the open.

4. The Shovel Man

ON the street
    Slung on the shoulder is a handle half-way across,
Tied in a big knot on the scoop of cast iron
Are the overalls faded from sun and rain in the ditches;
Spatter of dry clay sticking yellow on his left sleeve
        And a flimsy shirt open at the throat,
        I know him for a shovel man,
        A dago working for a dollar six bits a day
And a dark-eyed woman in the old country dreams of
    him for one of the world's ready men with a pair
    of fresh lips and a kiss better than all the wild
    grapes that ever grew in Tuscany.

5. A Teamster's Farewell

Sobs En Route to a Penitentiary

GOOD-BYE now to the streets and the clash of
    wheels and locking hubs,
The sun coming on the brass buckles and harness
    knobs,
The muscles of the horses sliding under their heavy
    haunches,
Good-bye now to the traffic policeman and his whistle,
The smash of the iron hoofs on the stones,
All the crazy wonderful slamming roar of the street—
O God, there's noises I'm going to be hungry for.

6. Fish Crier

I KNOW a Jew fish crier down on Maxwell Street,
with a voice like a north wind blowing over corn
stubble in January.
He dangles herring before prospective customers evinc-
ing a joy identical with that of Pavlova dancing.
His face is that of a man terribly glad to be selling
fish, terribly glad that God made fish, and cus-
tomers to whom he may call his wares from a
pushcart.

7. Picnic Boat

SUNDAY night and the park policemen tell each
other it is dark as a stack of black cats on Lake
Michigan.

A big picnic boat comes home to Chicago from the
peach farms of Saugatuck.

Hundreds of electric bulbs break the night's darkness,
a flock of red and yellow birds with wings at a
standstill.

Running along the deck railings are festoons and leap-
ing in curves are loops of light from prow and
stern to the tall smokestacks.

Over the hoarse crunch of waves at my pier comes a
hoarse answer in the rhythmic oompa of the
brasses playing a Polish folk-song for the home-
comers.

8. Happiness

I ASKED professors who teach the meaning of life to
tell me what is happiness.
And I went to famous executives who boss the work
of thousands of men.
They all shook their heads and gave me a smile as
though I was trying to fool with them.
And then one Sunday afternoon I wandered out along
the Desplaines River
And I saw a crowd of Hungarians under the trees with
their women and children and a keg of beer
and an accordion.

9. Muckers

TWENTY men stand watching the muckers.
Stabbing the sides of the ditch
Where clay gleams yellow,
Driving the blades of their shovels
Deeper and deeper for the new gas mains,
Wiping sweat off their faces
With red bandannas.
The muckers work on . . . pausing . . . to pull
Their boots out of suckholes, where they slosh.

Of the twenty looking on
Ten murmur, 'Oh, it's a hell of a job,'
Ten others, 'Jesus, I wish I had the job.'

10.   Blacklisted

WHY shall I keep the old name?
What is a name anywhere anyway?
A name is a cheap thing all fathers and mothers leave
each child:
A job is a job and I want to live, so
Why does God Almighty or anybody else care whether
I take a new name to go by?

11. Child of the Romans

THE dago shovelman sits by the railroad track
    Eating a noon meal of bread and bologna.
        A train whirls by, and men and women at tables
        Alive with red roses and yellow jonquils,
        Eat steaks running with brown gravy,
        Strawberries and cream, éclairs and coffee.
The dago shovelman finishes the dry bread and
    bologna,
Washes it down with a dipper from the water-boy,
And goes back to the second half of a ten-hour day's
    work
Keeping the road-bed so the roses and jonquils
Shake hardly at all in the cut-glass vases
Standing slender on the tables in the dining-cars.

12. The Right to Grief

To Certain Poets About to Die

TAKE your fill of intimate remorse, perfumed
   sorrow,
Over the dead child of a millionaire,
And the pity of Death refusing any cheque on the
   bank
Which the millionaire might order his secretary to
   scratch off
And get cashed.

   Very well,
You for your grief and I for mine.
Let me have a sorrow my own if I want to.

I shall cry over the dead child of a stockyards hunky.
His job is sweeping blood off the floor.
He gets a dollar seventy cents a day when he works
And it's many tubs of blood he shoves out with a
   broom day by day.

Now his three-year-old daughter
Is in a white coffin that cost him a week's wages.
Every Saturday night he will pay the undertaker fifty
   cents till the debt is wiped out.

The hunky and his wife and the kids
Cry over the pinched face almost at peace in the white
   box.

The Right to Grief

They remember it was scrawny and ran up high
    doctor bills.
They are glad it is gone, for the rest of the family
    now will have more to eat and wear.

Yet before the majesty of Death they cry around the
    coffin
And wipe their eyes with red bandannas and sob when
    the priest says, 'God have mercy on us all.'

I have a right to feel my throat choke about this.
You take your grief and I mine—see?
To-morrow there is no funeral and the hunky goes
    back to his job sweeping blood off the floor at a
    dollar seventy cents a day.
All he does all day long is keep on shoving hog blood
    ahead of him with a broom.

13.   Mag

I WISH to God I never saw you, Mag.
  I wish you never quit your job and came along with
      me.
  I wish we never bought a licence and a white dress
  For you to get married in the day we ran off to a min-
      ister
  And told him we would love each other and take care
      of each other
  Always and always long as the sun and the rain lasts
      anywhere.
  Yes, I'm wishing now you lived somewhere away
      from here
  And I was a bum on the bumpers a thousand miles
      away dead broke.
      I wish the kids had never come
      And rent and coal and clothes to pay for
      And a grocery man calling for cash,
      Every day cash for beans and prunes.
      I wish to God I never saw you, Mag.
      I wish to God the kids had never come.

14. Onion Days

Mrs. GABRIELLE GIOVANNITTI comes along Peoria Street every morning at nine o'clock

With kindling wood piled on top of her head, her eyes looking straight ahead to find the way for her old feet.

Her daughter-in-law, Mrs. Pietro Giovannitti, whose husband was killed in a tunnel explosion through the negligence of a fellow-servant,

Works ten hours a day, sometimes twelve, picking onions for Jasper on the Bowmanville road.

She takes a street car at half-past five in the morning, Mrs. Pietro Giovannitti does,

And gets back from Jasper's with cash for her day's work, between nine and ten o'clock at night.

Last week she got eight cents a box, Mrs. Pietro Giovannitti, picking onions for Jasper,

But this week Jasper dropped the pay to six cents a box because so many women and girls were answering the ads in the *Daily News*.

Jasper belongs to an Episcopal church in Ravenswood and on certain Sundays

He enjoys chanting the Nicene Creed with his daughters on each side of him joining their voices with his.

If the preacher repeats old sermons of a Sunday, Jas-

44

per's mind wanders to his 700-acre farm and
how he can make it produce more efficiently.

And sometimes he speculates on whether he could
word an ad in the *Daily News* so it would bring
more women and girls out to his farm and re-
duce operating costs.

Mrs. Pietro Giovannitti is far from desperate about
life; her joy is in a child she knows will arrive
to her in three months.

And now while these are the pictures for to-day there
are other pictures of the Giovannitti people I
could give you for to-morrow,

And how some of them go to the county agent on
winter mornings with their baskets for beans
and corn meal and molasses.

I listen to fellows saying here's good stuff for a novel
or it might be worked up into a good play.

I say there's no dramatist living can put old Mrs.
Gabrielle Giovannitti into a play with that
kindling wood piled on top of her head coming
along Peoria Street nine o'clock in the morning.

15.   A Fence

NOW the stone house on the lake front is finished
and the workmen are beginning the fence.
The palings are made of iron bars with steel points
that can stab the life out of any man who falls
on them.
As a fence, it is a masterpiece, and will shut off the
rabble and all vagabonds and hungry men and
all wandering children looking for a place to
play.
Passing through the bars and over the steel points will
go nothing except Death and the Rain and To-
morrow.

16. Working Girls

THE working girls in the morning are going to
work—long lines of them afoot amid the down-
town stores and factories, thousands with little
brick-shaped lunches wrapped in newspapers
under their arms.

Each morning as I move through this river of young-
woman life I feel a wonder about where it is
all going, so many with a peach bloom of young
years on them and laughter of red lips and mem-
ories in their eyes of dances the night before and
plays and walks.

Green and grey streams run side by side in a river and
so here are always the others, those who have
been over the way, the women who know each
one the end of life's gamble for her, the mean-
ing and the clue, the how and the why of the
dances and the arms that passed around their
waists and the fingers that played in their hair.

Faces go by written over: 'I know it all, I know
where the bloom and the laughter go and I
have memories,' and the feet of these move
slower and they have wisdom where the others
have beauty.

So the green and the grey move in the early morning
on the downtown streets.

17. Mamie

MAMIE beat her head against the bars of a little
Indiana town and dreamed of romance and big
things off somewhere the way the railroad trains
all ran.

She could see the smoke of the engines get lost down
where the streaks of steel flashed in the sun and
when the newspapers came in on the morning
mail she knew there was a big Chicago far off,
where all the trains ran.

She got tired of the barber shop boys and the post
office chatter and the church gossip and the old
pieces the band played on the Fourth of July and
Decoration Day,

And sobbed at her fate and beat her head against the
bars and was going to kill herself,

When the thought came to her that if she was going
to die she might as well die struggling for a
clutch of romance among the streets of Chicago.

She has a job now at six dollars a week in the base-
ment of the Boston Store

And even now she beats her head against the bars in
the same old way and wonders if there is a bigger
place the railroads run to from Chicago where
maybe there is

romance
and big things
and real dreams
that never go smash.

18.   Personality

Musings of a Police Reporter in the Identification Bureau

YOU have loved forty women, but you have only one
thumb.

You have led a hundred secret lives, but you mark
only one thumb.

You go round the world and fight in a thousand wars
and win all the world's honours, but when you
come back home the print of the one thumb your
mother gave you is the same print of thumb you
had in the old home when your mother kissed
you and said good-bye.

Out of the whirling womb of time come millions of
men and their feet crowd the earth and they cut
one another's throats for room to stand and
among them all are not two thumbs alike.

Somewhere is a Great God of Thumbs who can tell
the inside story of this.

19.   Cumulatives

STORMS have beaten on this point of land
And ships gone to wreck here
        and the passers-by remember it
        with talk on the deck at night
        as they near it.

Fists have beaten on the face of this old prize-fighter
And his battles have held the sporting pages
        and on the street they indicate him with their
        right forefinger as one who once wore
        a championship belt.

A hundred stories have been published and a thousand
    rumoured
About why this tall dark man has divorced two beau-
    tiful young women
And married a third who resembles the first two
        and they shake their heads and say, 'There he
        goes,'
        when he passes in sunny weather or in rain
        along the city streets.

20. The Has-Been

A STONE face higher than six horses stood five thousand years gazing at the world seeming to clutch a secret.

A boy passes and throws a niggerhead that chips off the end of the nose from the stone face; he lets fly a mud ball that spatters the right eye and cheek of the old looker-on.

The boy laughs and goes whistling 'ee-ee-ee ee-ee-ee.' The stone face stands silent, seeming to clutch a secret.

21. Ice Handler

I KNOW an ice handler who wears a flannel shirt
with pearl buttons the size of a dollar,

And he lugs a hundred-pound hunk into a saloon ice-
box, helps himself to cold ham and rye bread,

Tells the bartender it's hotter than yesterday and
will be hotter yet to-morrow, by Jesus,

And is on his way with his head in the air and a hard
pair of fists.

He spends a dollar or so every Saturday night on a
two hundred pound woman who washes dishes
in the Hotel Morrison.

He remembers when the union was organized he broke
the noses of two scabs and loosened the nuts so
the wheels came off six different wagons one
morning, and he came around and watched the
ice melt in the street.

All he was sorry for was one of the scabs bit him on
the knuckles of the right hand so they bled when
he came around to the saloon to tell the boys
about it.

22. Jack

JACK was a swarthy, swaggering son-of-a-gun.
He worked thirty years on the railroad ten hours a
day, and his hands were tougher than sole
leather.
He married a tough woman and they had eight chil-
dren and the woman died and the children grew
up and went away and wrote the old man every
two years.
He died in the poorhouse sitting on a bench in the sun
telling reminiscences to other old men whose
women were dead and children scattered.
There was joy on his face when he died as there was
joy on his face when he lived—he was a
swarthy, swaggering son-of-a-gun.

23.   Fellow-Citizens

I DRANK musty ale at the Illinois Athletic Club with
the millionaire manufacturer of Green River
butter one night.

And his face had the shining light of an old-time
Quaker, he spoke of a beautiful daughter, and I
knew he had a peace and a happiness up his sleeve
somewhere.

Then I heard Jim Kirch make a speech to the Adver-
tising Association on the trade resources of South
America

And the way he lighted a three-for-a-nickel stogie
and cocked it at an angle regardless of the man-
ners of our best people,

I knew he had a clutch on a real happiness even
though some of the reporters on his newspaper
say he is the living double of Jack London's
Sea Wolf.

In the mayor's office the mayor himself told me he
was happy though it is a hard job to satisfy all
the office-seekers and eat all the dinners he is
asked to eat.

Down in Gilpin Place, near Hull House, was a man
with his jaw wrapped for a bad toothache,

And he had it all over the butter millionaire, Jim
Kirch and the mayor when it came to happiness.

He is a maker of accordions and guitars, and not only

54

makes them from start to finish, but plays them
after he makes them.

And he had a guitar of mahogany with a walnut bot-
tom he offered for seven dollars and a half if I
wanted it,

And another just like it, only smaller, for six dollars,
though he never mentioned the price till I asked
him,

And he stated the price in a sorry way, as though the
music and the make of an instrument count for
a million times more than the price in money.

I thought he had a real soul and knew a lot about God.

There was light in his eyes of one who has con-
quered sorrow in so far as sorrow is conquerable
or worth conquering.

Anyway he is the only Chicago citizen I was jealous
of that day.

He played a dance they play in some parts of Italy
when the harvest of grapes is over and the wine
presses are ready for work.

24. To a Contemporary Bunk-shooter

YOU come along . . . tearing your shirt . . . yell-
ing about Jesus.
Where do you get that stuff?
What do you know about Jesus?

Jesus had a way of talking soft and outside of a few
bankers and higher-ups among the con men of
Jerusalem everybody liked to have this Jesus
around because he never made any fake passes
and everything he said went and he helped the
sick and gave the people hope.

You come along squirting words at us, shaking your
fist and call us all dam fools so fierce the
froth slobbers over your lips . . . always blab-
bing we're all going to hell straight off and
you know all about it.

I've read Jesus' words. I know what he said. You
don't throw any scare into me. I've got your
number. I know how much you know about
Jesus.

He never came near clean people or dirty people but
they felt cleaner because he came along. It
was your crowd of bankers and business men and
lawyers hired the sluggers and murderers who
put Jesus out of the running.

To a Contemporary Bunkshooter

I say the same bunch backing you nailed the nails into
the hands of this Jesus of Nazareth. He had
lined up against him the same crooks and strong-
arm men now lined up with you paying your
way.

This Jesus was good to look at, smelled good, listened
good. He threw out something fresh and beau-
tiful from the skin of his body and the touch of
his hands wherever he passed along.

You slimy bunkshooter, you put a smut on every
human blossom in reach of your rotten breath
belching about hell-fire and hiccupping about
this Man who lived a clean life in Galilee.

When are you going to quit making the carpenters
build emergency hospitals for women and girls
driven crazy with wrecked nerves from your
gibberish about Jesus?—I put it to you again:
Where do you get that stuff? what do you know
about Jesus?

Go ahead and bust all the chairs you want to. Smash
a whole wagon-load of furniture at every per-
formance. Turn sixty somersaults and stand
on your nutty head. If it wasn't for the way
you scare the women and kids I'd feel sorry
for you and pass the hat.

I like to watch a good four-flusher work, but not
when he starts people puking and calling for
the doctors.

To a Contemporary Bunkshooter

I like a man that's got nerve and can pull off a great original performance, but you—you're only a bug-house pedlar of second-hand gospel—you're only shoving out a phoney imitation of the goods this Jesus wanted free as air and sunlight.

You tell people living in shanties Jesus is going to fix it up all right with them by giving them mansions in the skies after they're dead and the worms have eaten 'em.

You tell $6 a week department store girls all they need is Jesus; you take a steel trust wop, dead without having lived, grey and shrunken at forty years of age, and you tell him to look at Jesus on the cross and he'll be all right.

You tell poor people they don't need any more money on pay day and even if it's fierce to be out of a job, Jesus'll fix that up all right, all right—all they gotta do is take Jesus the way you say.

I'm telling you Jesus wouldn't stand for the stuff you're handing out. Jesus played it different. The bankers and lawyers of Jerusalem got their sluggers and murderers to go after Jesus just because Jesus wouldn't play their game. He didn't sit in with the big thieves.

I don't want a lot of gab from a bunkshooter in my religion.

I won't take my religion from any man who never

To a Contemporary Bunkshooter

works except with his mouth and never cherishes
    any memory except the face of the woman on
    the American silver dollar.
I ask you to come through and show me where you're
    pouring out the blood of your life.
I've been to this suburb of Jerusalem they call Gol-
    gotha, where they nailed Him, and I know if
    the story is straight it was real blood ran from
    His hands and the nail-holes, and it was real
    blood spurted in red drops where the spear of
    the Roman soldier rammed in between the ribs
    of this Jesus of Nazareth.

25. Skyscraper

BY day the skyscraper looms in the smoke and sun
and has a soul,
  Prairie and valley, streets of the city, pour people into
it and they mingle among its twenty floors and
are poured out again back to the streets, prairies
and valleys.
  It is the men and women, boys and girls so poured in
and out all day that give the building a soul of
dreams and thoughts and memories.
  (Dumped in the sea or fixed in a desert, who would
care for the building or speak its name or ask
a policeman the way to it?)

  Elevators slide on their cables and tubes catch letters
and parcels and iron pipes carry gas and water in
and sewage out.
  Wires climb with secrets, carry light and carry words,
and tell terrors and profits and loves—curses of
men grappling plans of business and questions of
women in plots of love.

  Hour by hour the caissons reach down to the rock of
the earth and hold the building to a turning
planet.
  Hour by hour the girders play as ribs and reach out
and hold together the stone walls and floors.

Skyscraper

Hour by hour the hand of the mason and the stuff of
   the mortar clinch the pieces and parts to the shape
   an architect voted.
Hour by hour the sun and the rain, the air and the
   rust, and the press of time running into centuries,
   play on the building inside and out and use it.

Men who sunk the pilings and mixed the mortar are
   laid in graves where the wind whistles a wild
   song without words
And so are men who strung the wires and fixed the
   pipes and tubes and those who saw it rise floor
   by floor.
Souls of them all are here, even the hod carrier beg-
   ging at back doors hundreds of miles away and
   the bricklayer who went to state's prison for
   shooting another man while drunk.
(One man fell from a girder and broke his neck at
   the end of a straight plunge—he is here—his
   soul has gone into the stones of the building.)

On the office doors from tier to tier—hundreds of
   names and each name standing for a face written
   across with a dead child, a passionate lover, a
   driving ambition for a million dollar business or
   a lobster's ease of life.

Behind the signs on the doors they work and the
   walls tell nothing from room to room.
Ten-dollar-a-week stenographers take letters from

corporation officers, lawyers, efficiency engineers, and tons of letters go bundled from the building to all ends of the earth.

Smiles and tears of each office girl go into the soul of the building just the same as the master-men who rule the building.

Hands of clocks turn to noon hours and each floor empties its men and women who go away and eat and come back to work.

Toward the end of the afternoon all work slackens and all jobs go slower as the people feel day closing on them.

One by one the floors are emptied . . . The uniformed elevator men are gone. Pails clang . . . Scrubbers work, talking in foreign tongues. Broom and water and mop clean from the floors human dust and spit, and machine grime of the day.

Spelled in electric fire on the roof are words telling miles of houses and people where to buy a thing for money. The sign speaks till midnight.

Darkness on the hallways. Voices echo. Silence holds . . . Watchmen walk slow from floor to floor and try the doors. Revolvers bulge from their hip pockets . . . Steel safes stand in corners. Money is stacked in them.

A young watchman leans at a window and sees the lights of barges butting their way across a har-

bour, nets of red and white lanterns in a rail-
road yard, and a span of glooms splashed with
lines of white and blurs of crosses and clusters
over the sleeping city.

By night the skyscraper looms in the smoke and the
stars and has a soul.

26. Fog

THE fog comes
on little cat feet.

It sits looking
over harbour and city
on silent haunches
and then moves on.

27. Graves

I DREAMED one man stood against a thousand,
One man damned as a wrongheaded fool.
One year and another he walked the streets,
And a thousand shrugs and hoots
Met him in the shoulders and mouths he passed.

He died alone
And only the undertaker came to his funeral.

Flowers grow over his grave anod in the wind,
And over the graves of the thousand, too,
The flowers grow anod in the wind.

Flowers and the wind,
Flowers anod over the graves of the dead,
Petals of red, leaves of yellow, streaks of white,
Masses of purple sagging . . .
I love you and your great way of forgetting.

28. Aztec Mask

I WANTED a man's face looking into the jaws and
   throat of life
With something proud on his face, so proud no smash
   of the jaws,
No gulp of the throat leaves the face in the end
With anything else than the old proud look:
         Even to the finish, dumped in the dust,
         Lost among the used-up cinders,
         This face, men would say, is a flash,
         Is laid on bones taken from the ribs of the
            earth,
         Ready for the hammers of changing, chang-
            ing years,
         Ready for the sleeping, sleeping years of si-
            lence.
         Ready for the dust and fire and wind.
I wanted this face and I saw it to-day in an Aztec
   mask.
A cry out of storm and dark, a red yell and a purple
   prayer,
A beaten shape of ashes
            waiting the sunrise or night,
            something or nothing,
            proud-mouthed,
            proud-eyed gambler.

29. Shirt

I REMEMBER once I ran after you and tagged the
   fluttering shirt of you in the wind.
Once many days ago I drank a glassful of something
   and the picture of you shivered and slid on top
   of the stuff.
And again it was nobody else but you I heard in the
   singing voice of a careless humming woman.
One night when I sat with chums telling stories at a
   bonfire flickering red embers, in a language its
   own talking to a spread of white stars:
                It was you that slunk laughing
                in the clumsy staggering shadows.
Broken answers of remembrance let me know you are
   alive with a peering phantom face behind a door-
   way somewhere in the city's push and fury.
Or under a pack of moss and leaves waiting in silence
   under a twist of oaken arms ready as ever to run
   away again when I tag the fluttering shirt of you.

30. Aztec

YOU came from the Aztecs
   With a copper on your fore-arms
Tawnier than a sunset
Saying good-bye to an even river.

And I said, you remember,
Those fore-arms of yours
Were finer than bronzes
And you were glad.

                It was tears
And a path west
        and a home-going
        when I asked
Why there were scars of worn gold
Where a man's ring was fixed once
On your third finger.
              And I call you
To come back
        before the days are longer.

31. Theme in Yellow

I SPOT the hills
With yellow balls in autumn
I light the prairie cornfields
Orange and tawny gold clusters
And I am called pumpkins.
On the last of October
When dusk is fallen
Children join hands
And circle round me
Singing ghost songs
And love to the harvest moon;
I am a jack-o'-lantern
With terrible teeth
And the children know
I am fooling.

32. Harrison Street Court

I HEARD a woman's lips
Speaking to a companion
Say these words:

'A woman what hustles
Never keeps nothin'
For all her hustlin'.
Somebody always gets
What she goes on the street for.
If it ain't a pimp
It's a bull what gets it.
I been hustlin' now
Till I ain't much good any more.
I got nothin' to show for it.
Some man got it all,
Every night's hustlin' I ever did.'

33. Soiled Dove

LET us be honest; the lady was not a harlot until she married a corporation lawyer who picked her from a Ziegfeld chorus.

Before then she never took anybody's money and paid for her silk stockings out of what she earned singing and dancing.

She loved one man and he loved six women and the game was changing her looks, calling for more and more massage money and high coin for the beauty doctors.

Now she drives a long, underslung motor car all by herself, reads in the day's papers what her husband is doing to the inter-state commerce commission, requires a larger corsage from year to year, and wonders sometimes how one man is coming along with six women.

34. Jungheimer's

IN western fields of corn and northern timber lands,
    They talk about me, a saloon with a soul,
    The soft red lights, the long curving bar,
    The leather seats and dim corners,
    Tall brass spittoons, a nigger cutting ham,
And the painting of a woman half-dressed thrown
    reckless across a bed after a night of booze and
    riots.

35. Gone

EVERYBODY loved Chick Lorimer in our town
                    Far off.
            Everybody loved her.
So we all love a wild girl keeping a hold
            On a dream she wants.
Nobody knows now where Chick Lorimer went.
Nobody knows why she packed her trunk . . . a few
    old things
And is gone,
                    Gone with her little chin
                    Thrust ahead of her
                    And her soft hair blowing careless
                    From under a wide hat,
Dancer, singer, a laughing passionate lover.

Were there ten men or a hundred hunting Chick?
Were there five men or fifty with aching hearts?
            Everybody loved Chick Lorimer.
                    Nobody knows where she's gone.

36.   The Junk Man

I AM glad God saw Death
And gave Death a job taking care of all who are tired
of living:

When all the wheels in a clock are worn and slow and
the connections loose
And the clock goes on ticking and telling the wrong
time from hour to hour
And people around the house joke about what a bum
clock it is,
How glad the clock is when the big Junk Man drives
his wagon
Up to the house and puts his arms around the clock
and says:
　　　　　'You don't belong here,
　　　　　You gotta come
　　　　　Along with me,'
How glad the clock is then, when it feels the arms of
the Junk Man close around it and carry it away.

37. Prairie

I WAS born on the prairie, and the milk of its wheat, the red of its clover, the eyes of its women, gave me a song and a slogan.

Here the water went down, the icebergs slid with gravel, the gaps and the valleys hissed, and the black loam came, and the yellow sandy loam.

Here between the sheds of the Rocky Mountains and the Appalachians, here now a morning star fixes a fire sign over the timber claims and cow pastures, the corn belt, the cotton belt, the cattle ranches.

Here the grey geese go five hundred miles and back with a wind under their wings honking the cry for a new home.

Here I know I will hanker after nothing so much as one more sunrise or a sky moon of fire doubled to a river moon of water.

The prairie sings to me in the forenoon and I know in the night I rest easy in the prairie arms, on the prairie heart.

. . .

After the sunburn of the day
handling a pitchfork at a hayrack,
after the eggs and biscuit and coffee,
the pearl-grey haystacks
in the gloaming

Prairie

are cool prayers
to the harvest hands.

In the city among the walls the overland passenger train
    is choked and the pistons hiss and the wheels curse.
On the prairie the overland flits on phantom wheels and
    the sky and the soil between them muffle the pistons
    and cheer the wheels.

. . .

I am here when the cities are gone.
I am here before the cities come.
I nourished the lonely men on horses.
I will keep the laughing men who ride iron.
I am dust of men.

The running water babbled to the deer, the cottontail,
    the gopher.
You came in wagons, making streets and schools,
Kin of the axe and rifle, kin of the plough and horse
Singing *Yankee Doodle, Old Dan Tucker, Turkey in the
    Straw,*
You in the coonskin cap at a log house door hearing a
    lone wolf howl,
You at a sod house door reading the blizzards and chi-
    nooks let loose from Medicine Hat,
I am dust of your dust, as I am brother and mother
To the copper faces, the worker in flint and clay,
The singing women and their sons a thousand years ago
Marching single file the timber and the plain.

76

Prairie

I hold the dust of these amid changing stars.
I last while old wars are fought, while peace broods
    mother-like,
While new wars arise and the fresh killings of young
    men.
I fed the boys who went to France in great dark days.
Appomattox is a beautiful word to me and so is Valley
    Forge and the Marne and Verdun,
I who have seen the red births and the red deaths
Of sons and daughters, I take peace or war, I say nothing
    and wait.

Have you seen a red sunset drip over one of my corn-
    fields, the shore of night stars, the wave lines of
    dawn up a wheat valley?
Have you heard my threshing crews yelling in the chaff
    of a strawpile and the running wheat of the wagon-
    boards, my cornhuskers, my harvest hands hauling
    crops, singing dreams of women, worlds, horizons?

. . .

        Rivers cut a path on flat lands.
        The mountains stand up.
        The salt oceans press in
        And push on the coast lines.
        The sun, the wind, bring rain
        And I know what the rainbow writes
           across the east or west in a half-
           circle:
        A love-letter pledge to come again.

. . .

Prairie

Towns on the Soo Line,
Towns on the Big Muddy,
Laugh at each other for cubs
And tease as children.

Omaha and Kansas City, Minneapolis and St. Paul,
  sisters in a house together, throwing slang, growing
  up.
Towns in the Ozarks, Dakota wheat towns, Wichita,
  Peoria, Buffalo, sisters throwing slang, growing up.

. . .

Out of prairie-brown grass crossed with a streamer of
  wigwam smoke—out of a smoke pillar, a blue
  promise—out of wild ducks woven in greens and
  purples—
Here I saw a city rise and say to the peoples round world:
  Listen, I am strong, I know what I want.
Out of log houses and stumps—canoes stripped from tree
  sides—flatboats coaxed with an axe from the timber
  claims—in the years when the red and the white
  men met—the houses and streets rose.

A thousand red men cried and went away to new places
  for corn and women: a million white men came and
  put up skyscrapers, threw out rails and wires,
  feelers to the salt sea: now the smokestacks bite the
  skyline with stub teeth.

In an early year the call of a wild duck woven in greens

Prairie

and purples: now the riveter's chatter, the police
patrol, the song-whistle of the steamboat.

To a man across a thousand years I offer a handshake.
I say to him: Brother, make the story short, for the
stretch of a thousand years is short.

.   .   .

What brothers these in the dark?
What eaves of skyscrapers against a smoke moon?
These chimneys shaking on the lumber shanties
When the coal boats plough by on the river—
The hunched shoulders of the grain elevators—
The flame sprockets of the sheet steel mills
And the men in the rolling mills with their shirts off
Playing their flesh arms against the twisting wrists of
    steel:

        what brothers these
        in the dark
        of a thousand years?

.   .   .

A headlight searches a snowstorm.
A funnel of white lights shoots from over the pilot of
    the Pioneer Limited crossing Wisconsin.

In the morning hours, in the dawn,
The sun puts out the stars of the sky
And the headlight of the Limited train.

The fireman waves his hand to a country school
    teacher on a bobsled.

Prairie

A boy, yellow hair, red scarf and mittens, on the bob-
    sled, in his lunch box a pork chop sandwich and
    a V of gooseberry pie.

The horses fathom a snow to their knees.
Snow hats are on the rolling prairie hills.
The Mississippi bluffs wear snow hats.

Keep your hogs on changing corn and mashes of grain,
    O farmerman.
    Cram their insides till they waddle on short legs
    Under the drums of bellies, hams of fat.
    Kill your hogs with a knife slit under the ear.
    Hack them with cleavers.
    Hang them with hooks in the hind legs.

A wagonload of radishes on a summer morning.
Sprinkles of dew on the crimson-purple balls.
The farmer on the seat dangles the reins on the rumps
    of dapple-grey horses.
The farmer's daughter with a basket of eggs dreams
    of a new hat to wear to the county fair.

On the left- and right-hand side of the road,
            Marching corn—
I saw it knee high weeks ago—now it is head high—
    tassels of red silk creep at the ends of the ears.

I am the prairie, mother of men, waiting.

Prairie

They are mine, the threshing crews eating beefsteak, the
    farmboys driving steers to the railroad cattle pens.

They are mine, the crowds of people at a Fourth of July
    basket picnic, listening to a lawyer read the Declara-
    tion of Independence, watching the pinwheels and
    Roman candles at night, the young men and women
    two by two hunting the bypaths and kissing bridges.

They are mine, the horses looking over a fence in the
    frost of late October saying good-morning to the
    horses hauling wagons of rutabaga to market.

They are mine, the old zigzag rail fences, the new barb
    wire.

         . ·. .

The cornhuskers wear leather on their hands.

There is no let-up to the wind.

Blue bandannas are knotted at the ruddy chins.

Falltime and winter apples take on the smoulder of the
    five-o'clock November sunset: falltime, leaves, bon-
    fires, stubble, the old things go, and the earth is
    grizzled.

The land and the people hold memories, even among the
    anthills and the angleworms, among the toads and
    woodroaches—among gravestone writings rubbed
    out by the rain—they keep old things that never
    grow old.

The frost loosens corn husks.

Prairie

The sun, the rain, the wind
      loosen corn husks.
The men and women are helpers.
They are all cornhuskers together.
I see them late in the western evening
      in a smoke-red dust.

      . . .

The phantom of a yellow rooster flaunting a scarlet
    comb, on top of a dung pile crying hallelujah to
    the streaks of daylight,
The phantom of an old hunting dog nosing in the under-
    brush for muskrats, barking at a coon in a treetop
    at midnight, chewing a bone, chasing his tail round
    a corncrib,
The phantom of an old workhorse taking the steel point
    of a plough across a forty-acre field in spring,
    hitched to a harrow in summer, hitched to a wagon
    among cornshocks in fall,
These phantoms come into the talk and wonder of people
    on the front porch of a farmhouse late summer
    nights.
'The shapes that are gone are here,' said an old man
    with a cob pipe in his teeth one night in Kansas
    with a hot wind on the alfalfa.

      . . .

Look at six eggs
In a mocking-bird's nest.

Listen to six mocking-birds

Prairie

Flinging follies of O-be-joyful
Over the marshes and uplands.

Look at songs
Hidden in eggs.

.   .   ⁅.⁆

When the morning sun is on the trumpet-vine blossoms,
    sing at the kitchen pans: Shout All Over God's
    Heaven.
When the rain slants on the potato hills and the sun plays
    a silver shaft on the last shower, sing to the bush at
    the backyard fence: Mighty Lak a Rose.
When the icy sleet pounds on the storm windows and
    the house lifts to a great breath, sing for the outside
    hills: The Ole Sheep Done Know the Road, the
    Young Lambs Must Find the Way.

.   .   .

Spring slips back with a girl face calling always: 'Any
    new songs for me? Any new songs?'

O prairie girl, be lonely, singing, dreaming, waiting—
    your lover comes—your child comes—the years
    creep with toes of April rain on new-turned sod.
O prairie girl, whoever leaves you only crimson poppies
    to talk with, whoever puts a good-bye kiss on your
    lips and never comes back—
There is a song deep as the falltime redhaws, long as
    the layer of black loam we go to, the shine of the

morning star over the corn belt, the wave line of
dawn up a wheat valley.

O prairie mother, I am one of your boys.
I have loved the prairie as a man with a heart shot full
of pain over love.
Here I know I will hanker after nothing so much as one
more sunrise or a sky moon of fire doubled to a
river moon of water.

I speak of new cities and new people.
I tell you the past is a bucket of ashes.
I tell you yesterday is a wind gone down,
a sun dropped in the west.
I tell you there is nothing in the world
only an ocean of to-morrows,
a sky of to-morrows.

I am a brother of the cornhuskers who say
at sundown:
To-morrow is a day.

38. River Roads

LET the crows go by hawking their caw and caw
They have been swimming in midnights of coal mine
somewhere.
Let 'em hawk their caw and caw.

Let the woodpecker drum and drum on a hickory
stump.
He has been swimming in red and blue pools some-
where hundreds of years
And the blue has gone to his wings and the red has
gone to his head.
Let his red head drum and drum.

Let the dark pools hold the birds in a looking-glass.
And if the pool wishes, let it shiver to the blur of many
wings, old swimmers from old places.

Let the redwing streak a line of vermilion on the
green wood lines.
And the mist along the river fix its purple in lines of
a woman's shawl on lazy shoulders.

39. Prairie Waters by Night

CHATTER of birds two by two raises a night song joining a litany of running water—sheer waters showing the russet of old stones remembering many rains.

And the long willows drowse on the shoulders of the running water, and sleep from much music; joined songs of day-end, feathery throats and stony waters, in a choir chanting new psalms.

It is too much for the long willows when low laughter of a red moon comes down; and the willows drowse and sleep on the shoulders of the running water.

40. Early Moon

THE baby moon, a canoe, a silver papoose canoe, sails and sails in the Indian west.

A ring of silver foxes, a mist of silver foxes, sit and sit around the Indian moon.

One yellow star for a runner, and rows of blue stars for more runners, keep a line of watchers.

O foxes, baby moon, runners, you are the panel of memory, fire-white writing to-night of the Red Man's dreams.

Who squats, legs crossed and arms folded, matching its look against the moon-face, the star-faces, of the West?

Who are the Mississippi Valley ghosts, of copper fore-heads, riding wiry ponies in the night?—no bri-dles, love-arms on the pony necks, riding in the night a long old trail?

Why do they always come back when the silver foxes sit around the early moon, a silver papoose, in the Indian west?

41. Laughing Corn

THERE was a high majestic fooling
   Day before yesterday in the yellow corn.

And day after to-morrow in the yellow corn
There will be high majestic fooling.

The ears ripen in late summer
And come on with a conquering laughter,
Come on with a high and conquering laughter.

The long-tailed blackbirds are hoarse.
One of the smaller blackbirds chitters on a stalk
And a spot of red is on its shoulder
And I never heard its name in my life.

Some of the ears are bursting.
A white juice works inside.
Cornsilk creeps in the end and dangles in the wind.
Always—I never knew it any other way—
The wind and the corn talk things over together.
And the rain and the corn and the sun and the corn
Talk things over together.

Over the road is the farmhouse.
The siding is white and a green blind is slung loose.
It will not be fixed till the corn is husked.
The farmer and his wife talk things over together.

42. Falltime

GOLD of a ripe oat straw, gold of a southwest moon,
  Canada thistle blue and flimmering larkspur blue,
  Tomatoes shining in the October sun with red hearts,
  Shining five and six in a row on a wooden fence,
  Why do you keep wishes on your faces all day long,
  Wishes like women with half-forgotten lovers going
      to new cities?
What is there for you in the birds, the birds, the
      birds, crying down on the north wind in Septem-
      ber, acres of birds spotting the air going south?
Is there something finished?   And some new begin-
      ning on the way?

89

43.　Illinois Farmer

BURY this old Illinois farmer with respect.
He slept the Illinois nights of his life after days of
　　work in Illinois cornfields.
Now he goes on a long sleep.
The wind he listened to in the cornsilk and the tassels,
　　the wind that combed his red beard zero morn-
　　ings when the snow lay white on the yellow ears
　　in the bushel basket at the corncrib,
The same wind will now blow over the place here
　　where his hands must dream of Illinois corn.

44. Hits and Runs

I REMEMBER the Chillicothe ball players grappling the Rock Island ball players in a sixteen-inning game ended by darkness.

And the shoulders of the Chillicothe players were a red smoke against the sundown and the shoulders of the Rock Island players were a yellow smoke against the sundown.

And the umpire's voice was hoarse calling balls and strikes and outs, and the umpire's throat fought in the dust for a song.

45. Village in late Summer

LIPS half-willing in a doorway.
Lips half-singing at a window.
Eyes half-dreaming in the walls.
Feet half-dancing in a kitchen.
Even the clocks half-yawn the hours
And the farmers make half-answers.

46. Sunset from Omaha Hotel Window

INTO the blue river hills
The red sun runners go
And the long sand changes
And to-day is a goner
And to-day is not worth haggling over.

Here in Omaha
The gloaming is bitter
As in Chicago
Or Kenosha.

The long sand changes.
To-day is a goner.
Time knocks in another brass nail.
Another yellow plunger shoots the dark.

Constellations
Wheeling over Omaha
As in Chicago
Or Kenosha.

The long sand is gone
and all the talk is stars.
They circle in a dome over Nebraska.

93

47. Still Life

COOL your heels on the rail of an observation car.
Let the engineer open her up for ninety miles an
hour.

Take in the prairie right and left, rolling land and
new hay crops, swaths of new hay laid in the sun.

A grey village flecks by and the horses hitched in front
of the post-office never blink an eye.

A barnyard and fifteen Holstein cows, dabs of white
on a black wall map, never blink an eye.

A signalman in a tower, the outpost of Kansas City,
keeps his place at a window with the serenity of a
bronze statue on a dark night when lovers pass
whispering.

48. Band Concert

BAND concert public square Nebraska city. Flowing and circling dresses, summer-white dresses. Faces, flesh tints flung like sprays of cherry blossoms. And gigglers, God knows, gigglers, rivalling the pony whinnies of the Livery Stable Blues.

Cowboy rags and nigger rags. And boys driving sorrel horses hurl a cornfield laughter at the girls in dresses, summer-white dresses. Amid the cornet staccato and the tuba oompa, gigglers, God knows, gigglers daffy with life's razzle dazzle.

Slow good-night melodies and Home Sweet Home. And the snare drummer bookkeeper in a hardware store nods hello to the daughter of a railroad conductor—a giggler, God knows, a giggler—and the summer-white dresses filter fanwise out of the public square.

The crushed strawberries of ice cream soda places, the night wind in cottonwoods and willows, the lattice shadows of doorsteps and porches, these know more of the story.

49. Three Pieces on the Smoke of Autumn

SMOKE of autumn is on it all.
The streamers loosen and travel.
The red west is stopped with a grey haze.
They fill the ash trees, they wrap the oaks,
They make a long-tailed rider
In the pocket of the first, the earliest evening star.

. . .

Three muskrats swim west on the Desplaines River.

There is a sheet of red ember glow on the river; it is
dusk; and the muskrats one by one go on patrol
routes west.

Around each slippery padding rat, a fan of ripples; in
the silence of dusk a faint wash of ripples, the
padding of the rats going west, in a dark and
shivering river gold.

(A newspaper in my pocket says the Germans pierce
the Italian line; I have letters from poets and
sculptors in Greenwich Village; I have letters
from an ambulance man in France and an
I.W.W. man in Vladivostok.)

Three Pieces on the Smoke of Autumn

I lean on an ash and watch the lights fall, the red ember
    glow, and three muskrats swim west in a fan of
    ripples on a sheet of river gold.

. . .

Better the blue silence and the grey west,
The autumn mist on the river,
And not any hate and not any love,
And not anything at all of the keen and the deep:
Only the peace of a dog head on a barn floor,
And the new corn shovelled in bushels
And the pumpkins brought from the corn rows,
Umber lights of the dark,
Umber lanterns of the loam dark.

Here a dog head dreams.
Not any hate, not any love.
Not anything but dreams.
Brother of dusk and umber.

50.   Localities

WAGON WHEEL GAP is a place I never saw,
  And Red Horse Gulch and the chutes of Cripple
    Creek.

Red-shirted miners picking in the sluices,
Gamblers with red neckties in the night streets,
The fly-by-night towns of Bull Frog and Skiddoo,
The night-cool limestone white of Death Valley,
The straight drop of eight hundred feet
From a shelf road in the Hasiampa Valley:
Men and places they are I never saw.

I have seen three White Horse taverns,
One in Illinois, one in Pennsylvania,
One in a timber-hid road of Wisconsin.

I bought cheese and crackers
Between sun showers in a place called White Pigeon
Nestling with a blacksmith shop, a post-office,
And a berry-crate factory, where four roads cross.

On the Pecatonica River near Freeport
I have seen boys run barefoot in the leaves
Throwing clubs at the walnut trees
In the yellow-and-gold of autumn,

Localities

And there was a brown mash dry on the inside of their
    hands.
On the Cedar Fork Creek of Knox County
I know how the fingers of late October
Loosen the hazel nuts.
I know the brown eyes of half-open hulls.
I know boys named Lindquist, Swanson, Hildebrand.
I remember their cries when the nuts were ripe.
And some are in machine shops; some are in the navy;
And some are not on payrolls anywhere.
Their mothers are through waiting for them to come
    home.

51. Caboose Thoughts

IT'S going to come out all right—do you know?
The sun, the birds, the grass—they know.
They get along—and we'll get along.

Some days will be rainy and you will sit waiting
And the letter you wait for won't come,
And I will sit watching the sky tear off grey and grey
And the letter I wait for won't come.

There will be ac-ci-dents.
I know ac-ci-dents are coming.
Smash-ups, signals wrong, washouts, trestles rotten,
Red and yellow ac-ci-dents.
But somehow and somewhere the end of the run
The train gets put together again
And the caboose and the green tail lights
Fade down the right of way like a new white hope.

I never heard a mocking bird in Kentucky
Spilling its heart in the morning.

I never saw the snow on Chimborazo.
It's a high white Mexican hat, I hear.

I never had supper with Abe Lincoln.
Nor a dish of soup with Jim Hill.

Caboose Thoughts

But I've been around.
I know some of the boys here who can go a little.
I know girls good for a burst of speed any time.

I heard Williams and Walker
Before Walker died in the bughouse.

I knew a mandolin player
Working in a barber shop in an Indiana town,
And he thought he had a million dollars.

I knew a hotel girl in Des Moines.
She had eyes; I saw her and said to myself
The sun rises and her heart went pit-a-pat.
We took away the money for a prize waltz at a Brother-
    hood dance.
She had eyes; she was safe as the bridge over the Mis-
    sissippi at Burlington; I married her.

Last summer we took the cushions going west.
Pike's peak is a big old stone, believe me.
It's fastened down; something you can count on.

It's going to come out all right—do you know?
The sun, the birds, the grass—they know.
They get along—and we'll get along.

52. Potato Blossom Songs and Jigs

RUM tiddy um,
   tiddy um,
tiddy um tum tum.

My knees are loose-like, my feet want to sling their
   selves.
I feel like tickling you under the chin—honey—and
   a-asking: Why Does a Chicken Cross the Road?
When the hens are a-laying eggs, and the roosters pluck-
   pluck-put-akut and you—honey—put new potatoes
   and gravy on the table, and there ain't too much
   rain or too little:
         Say, why do I feel so gabby?
         Why do I want to holler all over the place?

      . . .

Do you remember I held empty hands to you
   and I said all is yours
   the handfuls of nothing?

      . . .

I ask you for white blossoms.
I bring a concertina after sunset under the apple trees.
I bring out 'The Spanish Cavalier' and 'In the Gloam-
   ing, O My Darling.'

The orchard here is near and home-like.
The oats in the valley run a mile.
Between are the green and marching potato vines.

Potato Blossom Songs and Jigs

The lightning bugs go criss-cross carrying a zigzag of
fire: the potato bugs are asleep under their stiff
and yellow-striped wings: here romance stutters to
the western stars, 'Excuse . . . me . . .'

. . .

Old foundations of rotten wood.
An old barn done-for and out of the wormholes ten-
legged roaches shook up and scared by sunlight.
So a pickaxe digs a long tooth with a short memory.
Fire cannot eat this rubbish till it has lain in the sun.

. . .

The story lags.
The story has no connections.
The story is nothing but a lot of banjo plinka planka
plunks.

The roan horse is young and will learn: the roan horse
buckles into harness and feels the foam on the col-
lar at the end of a haul: the roan horse points four
legs to the sky and rolls in the red clover: the roan
horse has a rusty jag of hair between the ears hang-
ing to a white star between the eyes.

. . .

In Burlington long ago
And later again in Ashtabula
I said to myself:
    I wonder how far Ophelia went with Hamlet.
What else was there Shakespeare never told?

Potato Blossom Songs and Jigs

There must have been something.
If I go bugs I want to do it like Ophelia.
There was class to the way she went out of her head.

. . .

Does a famous poet eat watermelon?
Excuse me, ask me something easy.
I have seen farmhands with their faces in fried catfish
on a Monday morning.

And the Japanese, two-legged like us,
The Japanese bring slices of watermelon into pictures.
The black seeds make oval polka dots on the pink meat.

Why do I always think of niggers and buck-and-wing
dancing whenever I see watermelon?

Summer mornings on the docks I walk among bushel
peach baskets piled ten feet high.
Summer mornings I smell new wood and the river wind
along with peaches.
I listen to the steamboat whistle hong-honging, hong-
honging across the town.
And once I saw a teameo straddling a street with a hay-
rack load of melons.

. . .

Niggers play banjos because they want to.
The explanation is easy.

It is the same as why people pay fifty cents for tickets to

a policemen's masquerade ball or a grocers-and-
butchers' picnic with a fat man's foot race.
It is the same as why boys buy a nickel's worth of pea-
nuts and eat them and then buy another nickel's
worth.
Newsboys shooting craps in a back alley have a fugitive
understanding of the scientific principle involved.
The jockey in a yellow satin shirt and scarlet boots, rid-
ing a sorrel pony at the county fair, has a grasp
of the theory.
It is the same as why boys go running lickety-split
away from a school-room geography lesson
in April when the crawfishes come out
and the young frogs are calling
and the pussywillows and the cat-tails
know something about geography themselves.

. . .

I ask you for white blossoms.
I offer you memories and people.
I offer you a fire zigzag over the green and marching
vines.
I bring a concertina after supper under the home-like
apple trees.
I make up songs about things to look at:
potato blossoms in summer night mist filling the
garden with white spots;
a cavalryman's yellow silk handkerchief stuck in a
flannel pocket over the left side of the shirt,
over the ventricles of blood, over the pumps of
the heart.

Potato Blossom Songs and Jigs

Bring a concertina after sunset under the apple
    trees.
Let romance stutter to the western stars, 'Excuse . . .
    me . . .'

53.   Manitoba Childe Roland

LAST night a January wind was ripping at the shingles over our house and whistling a wolf song under the eaves.

I sat in a leather rocker and read to a six-year-old girl the Browning poem, *Childe Roland to the Dark Tower Came.*

And her eyes had the haze of autumn hills and it was beautiful to her and she could not understand.

A man is crossing a big prairie, says the poem, and nothing happens—and he goes on and on—and it's all lonesome and empty and nobody home.

And he goes on and on—and nothing happens—and he comes on a horse's skull, dry bones of a dead horse—and you know more than ever it's all lonesome and empty and nobody home.

And the man raises a horn to his lips and blows—he fixes a proud neck and forehead toward the empty sky and the empty land—and blows one last wonder-cry.

And as the shuttling automatic memory of man clicks

107

Manitoba Childe Roland

off its results willy-nilly and inevitable as the
snick of a mouse-trap or the trajectory of a 42-
centimetre projectile,

I flash to the form of a man to his hips in snow drifts
of Manitoba and Minnesota—in the sled Derby
run from Winnipeg to Minneapolis.

He is beaten in the race the first day out of Winnipeg—
the lead dog is eaten by four team mates—and the
man goes on and on—running while the other racers
ride—running while the other racers sleep—

Lost in a blizzard twenty-four hours, repeating a circle
of travel hour after hour—fighting the dogs who
dig holes in the snow and whimper for sleep—push-
ing on—running and walking five hundred miles
to the end of the race—almost a winner—one toe
frozen, feet blistered and frost-bitten.

And I know why a thousand young men of the North-
west meet him in the finishing miles and yell cheers
—I know why judges of the race call him a winner
and give him a special prize even though he is a
loser.

I know he kept under his shirt and around his thudding
heart amid the blizzards of five hundred miles that

one last wonder-cry of Childe Roland—and I told
the six-year-old girl all about it.

And while the January wind was ripping at the shingles
and whistling a wolf song under the eaves, her eyes
had the haze of autumn hills and it was beautiful
to her and she could not understand.

54. Wilderness

THERE is a wolf in me . . . fangs pointed for tearing gashes . . . a red tongue for raw meat . . . and the hot lapping of blood—I keep this wolf because the wilderness gave it to me and the wilderness will not let it go.

There is a fox in me . . . a silver-grey fox . . . I sniff and guess . . . I pick things out of the wind and air . . . I nose in the dark night and take sleepers and eat them and hide the feathers . . . I circle and loop and double-cross.

There is a hog in me—a snout and a belly . . . a machinery for eating and grunting . . . a machinery for sleeping satisfied in the sun—I got this too from the wilderness and the wilderness will not let it go.

There is a fish in me . . . I know I came from salt-blue water-gates . . . I scurried with shoals of herring . . . I blew waterspouts with porpoises . . . before land was . . . before the water went down . . . before Noah . . . before the first chapter of Genesis.

There is a baboon in me . . . clambering-clawed

Wilderness

. . . dog-faced . . . yawping a galoot's hunger
. . . hairy under the armpits . . . here are the
hawk-eyed hankering men . . . here are the blond
and blue-eyed women . . . here they hide curled
asleep waiting . . . ready to snarl and kill . . .
ready to sing and give milk . . . waiting—I keep
the baboon because the wilderness says so.

There is an eagle in me and a mocking-bird . . . and
the eagle flies among the Rocky Mountains of my
dreams and fights among the Sierra crags of what
I want . . . and the mocking-bird warbles in the
early forenoon before the dew is gone, warbles in
the underbrush of my Chattanoogas of hope, gushes
over the blue Ozark foothills of my wishes—And
I got the eagle and the mocking-bird from the wil-
derness.

O, I got a zoo, I got a menagerie, inside my ribs, under
my bony head, under my red-valve heart—and I
got something else: it is a man-child heart, a
woman-child heart: it is a father and mother and
lover: it came from God-Knows-Where: it is going
to God-Knows-Where—For I am the keeper of
the zoo: I say yes and no: I sing and kill and work:
I am a pal of the world: I came from the wilder-
ness.

55. Chicago Poet

I SALUTED a nobody.
I saw him in a looking-glass.
He smiled—so did I.
He crumpled the skin on his forehead,
    frowning—so did I.
Everything I did he did.
I said, 'Hello, I know you.'
And I was a liar to say so.

Ah, this looking-glass man!
Liar, fool, dreamer, play-actor,
Soldier, dusty drinker of dust—
Ah! he will go with me
Down the dark stairway
When nobody else is looking,
When everybody else is gone.

He locks his elbow in mine,
I lose all—but not him.

56. Memoir of a Proud Boy

HE lived on the wings of storm.
The ashes are in Chihuahua.

Out of Ludlow and coal towns in Colorado
Sprang a vengeance of Slav miners, Italians, Scots,
        Cornishmen, Yanks.
Killings ran under the spoken commands of this boy
With eighty men and rifles on a hogback mountain.

They killed swearing to remember
The shot and charred wives and children
In the burnt camp of Ludlow,
And Louis Tikas, the laughing Greek,
Plugged with a bullet, clubbed with a gun butt.

As a home war
It held the nation a week
And one or two million men stood together
And swore by the retribution of steel.

It was all accidental.
He lived flecking lint off coat lapels
Of men he talked with.
He kissed the miners' babies
And wrote a Denver paper
Of picket silhouettes on a mountain line.

Memoir of a Proud Boy

He had no mother but Mother Jones
Crying from a jail window of Trinidad:
'All I want is room enough to stand
And shake my fist at the enemies of the human race.'

Named by a grand jury as a murderer
He went to Chihuahua, forgot his old Scotch name,
Smoked cheroots with Pancho Villa
And wrote letters of Villa as a rock of the people.
How can I tell how Don Magregor went?

Three riders emptied lead into him.
He lay on the main street of an inland town.
A boy sat near all day throwing stones
To keep pigs away.

The Villa men buried him in a pit
With twenty Carranzistas.

There is drama in that point . . .
. . . the boy and the pigs.
Griffith would make a movie of it to fetch sobs.
Victor Herbert would have the drums whirr
In a weave with a high fiddle-string's single clamour.

'And the muchacho sat there all day throwing stones
To keep the pigs away,' wrote Gibbons to the *Tribune*.

Somewhere in Chihuahua or Colorado
Is a leather bag of poems and short stories.

57. Bilbea

(From tablet writing, Babylonian excavations of 4th millennium B.C.)

BILBEA, I was in Babylon on Saturday night.
I saw nothing of you anywhere.
I was at the old place and the other girls were there,
    but no Bilbea.

Have you gone to another house? or city?
Why don't you write?
I was sorry. I walked home half-sick.

Tell me how it goes.
Send me some kind of a letter
And take care of yourself.

58. Southern Pacific

HUNTINGTON sleeps in a house six feet long.
Huntington dreams of railroads he built and
owned,
Huntington dreams of ten thousand men saying: Yes,
sir.

Blithery sleeps in a house six feet long.
Blithery dreams of rails and ties he laid.
Blithery dreams of saying to Huntington: Yes, sir.

Huntington,
Blithery, sleep in houses six feet long.

59. Portrait of a Motor Car

IT'S a lean car . . . a long-legged dog of a car
. . . a grey-ghost eagle car.
The feet of it eat the dirt of a road . . . the wings
of it eat the hills.
Danny the driver dreams of it when he sees women in
red skirts and red socks in his sleep.
It is in Danny's life and runs in the blood of him
. . . a lean grey-ghost car.

60. Buffalo Bill

BOY heart of Johnny Jones—aching to-day?
Aching, and Buffalo Bill in town?
Buffalo Bill and ponies, cowboys, Indians?

Some of us know
All about it, Johnny Jones.

Buffalo Bill is a slanting look of the eyes,
  A slanting look under a hat on a horse.
He sits on a horse and a passing look is fixed
  On Johnny Jones, you and me, barelegged,
A slanting, passing, careless look under a hat on a
  horse.

Go clickety-clack, O pony hoofs along the street.
Come on and slant your eyes again, O Buffalo Bill.
Give us again the ache of our boy hearts.
Fill us again with the red love of prairies, dark nights,
  lonely wagons, and the crack-crack of rifles
  sputtering flashes into an ambush.

61. Singing Nigger

YOUR bony head, Jazbo, O dock walloper,
Those grappling hooks, those wheelbarrow handlers,
The dome and the wings of you, nigger,
The red roof and the door of you,
I know where your songs came from.
I know why God listens to your, 'Walk all over
God's Heaven.'
I heard you shooting craps, 'My baby's going to have
a new dress.'
I heard you in the cinders, 'I'm going to live anyhow
until I die.'
I saw five of you with a can of beer on a summer
night and I listened to the five of you harmoniz-
ing six ways to sing, 'Way Down Yonder in the
Cornfield.'
I went away asking where I come from.

62. Always the Mob

JESUS emptied the devils of one man into forty hogs
and the hogs took the edge of a high rock and
dropped off and down into the sea: a mob.

The sheep on the hills of Australia, blundering four-
footed in the sunset mist to the dark, they go one
way, they hunt one sleep, they find one pocket of
grass for all.

Karnak? Pyramids? Sphinx paws tall as a coolie?
Tombs kept for kings and sacred cows? A mob.

Young roast pigs and naked dancing girls of Belshaz-
zar, the room where a thousand sat guzzling
when a hand wrote: Mene, mene, tekel, up-
harsin? A mob.

The honeycomb of green that won the sun as the
Hanging Gardens of Nineveh, flew to its shape
at the hands of a mob that followed the fingers
of Nebuchadnezzar: a move of one hand and
one plan.

Stones of a circle of hills at Athens, staircases of a
mountain in Peru, scattered clans of marble
dragons in China: each a mob on the rim of a
sunrise: hammers and wagons have them now.

Always the Mob

Locks and gates of Panama? The Union Pacific crossing deserts and tunnelling mountains? The Woolworth on land and the *Titanic* at sea? Lighthouses blinking a coast line from Labrador to Key West? Pig iron bars piled on a barge whistling in a fog off Sheboygan? A mob: hammers and wagons have them to-morrow.

The mob? A typhoon tearing loose an island from thousand-year moorings and bastions, shooting a volcanic ash with a fire tongue that licks up cities and peoples. Layers of worms eating rocks and forming loam and valley floors for potatoes, wheat, watermelons.

The mob? A jag of lightning, a geyser, a gravel mass loosening . . .

The mob . . . kills or builds . . . the mob is Attila or Ghengis Khan, the mob is Napoleon, Lincoln.

I am born in the mob—I die in the mob—the same goes for you—I don't care who you are.

I cross the sheets of fire in No Man's Land for you, my brother—I slip a steel tooth into your throat, you my brother—I die for you and I kill you—It is a twisted and gnarled thing, a crimson wool:

> One more arch of stars,
> In the night of our mist,
> In the night of our tears.

63.   Interior

IN the cool of the night time
The clocks pick off the points
And the mainsprings loosen.
They will need winding.
One of these days . . .
        they will need winding.

Rabelais in red boards,
Walt Whitman in green,
Hugo in ten-cent paper covers,
Here they stand on shelves
In the cool of the night time
And there is nothing . . .
To be said against them . . .
Or for them . . .
In the cool of the night time
And the clocks.

A man in pigeon-grey pyjamas.
The open window begins at his feet
And goes taller than his head.
Eight feet high is the pattern.

Moon and mist make an oblong layout.
Silver at the man's bare feet.

Interior

He swings one foot in a moon silver.
And it costs nothing.

One more day of bread and work.
One more day . . . so much rags . . .
The man barefoot in moon silver
Mutters 'You' and 'You'
To things hidden
In the cool of the night time,
In Rabelais, Whitman, Hugo,
In an oblong of moon mist.

Out from the window . . . prairie-lands.
Moon mist whitens a golf ground.
White yet is a limestone quarry.
The crickets keep on chirring.

Switch engines of the Great Western
Sidetrack box cars, make up trains
For Weehawken, Oskaloosa, Saskatchewan;
The cattle, the coal, the corn, must go
In the night . . . on the prairie-lands.

Chuff-chuff go the pulses.
They beat in the cool of the night time.
Chuff-chuff and chuff-chuff . . .
These heartbeats travel the night a mile
And touch the moon silver at the window

Interior

And the bones of the man.
It costs nothing.

Rabelais in red boards,
Whitman in green,
Hugo in ten-cent paper covers,
Here they stand on shelves
In the cool of the night time
And the clocks.

64. Palladiums

IN the newspaper office—who are the spooks?
Who wears the mythic coat invisible?

Who pussyfoots from desk to desk
                    with a speaking forefinger?
Who gumshoes amid the copy paper
                    with a whispering thumb?

Speak softly—the sacred cows may hear.
Speak easy—the sacred cows must be fed.

65. Clocks

HERE is a face that says half-past seven the same
way whether a murder or a wedding goes on,
whether a funeral or a picnic crowd passes.

A tall one I know at the end of a hallway broods in
shadows and is watching booze eat out the insides
of the man of the house; it has seen five hopes
go in five years: one woman, one child, and
three dreams.

A little one carried in a leather box by an actress rides
with her to hotels and is under her pillow in a
sleeping-car between one-night stands.

One hoists a phiz over a railroad station: it points
numbers to people a quarter-mile away, who be-
lieve it when other clocks fail.

And of course . . . there are wrist watches over
the pulses of airmen eager to go to France.

66. Psalm of Those who Go Forth before Daylight

THE policeman buys shoes slow and careful; the teamster buys gloves slow and careful; they take care of their feet and hands; they live on their feet and hands.

The milkman never argues; he works alone and no one speaks to him; the city is asleep when he is on the job; he puts a bottle on six hundred porches and calls it a day's work; he climbs two hundred wooden stairways; two horses are company for him; he never argues.

The rolling-mill men and the sheet-steel men are brothers of cinders; they empty cinders out of their shoes after the day's work; they ask their wives to fix burnt holes in the knees of their trousers; their necks and ears are covered with a smut; they scour their necks and ears; they are brothers of cinders.

67. Horses and Men in Rain

LET us sit by a hissing steam radiator a winter's day,
grey wind pattering frozen raindrops on the
window,
And let us talk about milk wagon drivers and grocery
delivery boys.

Let us keep our feet in wool slippers and mix hot
punches—and talk about mail carriers and mes-
senger boys slipping along the icy sidewalks.
Let us write of olden, golden days and hunters of the
Holy Grail and men called 'knights' riding
horses in the rain, in the cold frozen rain for
ladies they loved.

A roustabout hunched on a coal wagon goes by, icicles
drip on his hat rim, sheets of ice wrapping the
hunks of coal, the caravanserai a grey blur in
slant of rain.
Let us nudge the steam radiator with our wool slip-
pers and write poems of Launcelot, the hero,
and Roland, the hero, and all the olden golden
men who rode horses in the rain.

68. Near Keokuk

THIRTY-TWO Greeks are dipping their feet in a
    creek.
Sloshing their bare feet in a cool flow of clear water.
All one midsummer day ten hours the Greeks
        stand in leather shoes shovelling gravel.
Now they hold their toes and ankles
        to the drift of running water.
Then they go to the bunk cars
        and eat mulligan and prune sauce,
Smoke one or two pipefuls, look at the stars,
        tell smutty stories
About men and women they have known,
        countries they have seen,
Railroads they have built—
        and then the deep sleep of children.

69. Slants at Buffalo, New York

A FOREFINGER of stone, dreamed by a sculptor,
points to the sky.
It says: This way! this way!

Four lions snore in stone at the corner of the shaft.
They too are the dream of a sculptor.
They too say: This way! this way!

The street cars swing at a curve.
The middle-class passengers witness low life.
The car windows frame low life all day in pictures.

Two Italian cellar delicatessens
sell red and green peppers.
The Florida bananas furnish a burst of yellow.
The lettuce and the cabbage give a green.

Boys play marbles in the cinders.
The boys' hands need washing.
The boys are glad; they fight among each other.

A plank bridge leaps the Lehigh Valley railroad.
Then acres of steel rails, freight cars, smoke,
And then . . . the blue lake shore
. . . Erie with Norse blue eyes . . . and the white
sun.

70. Flat Lands

FLAT lands on the end of town where real estate
men are crying new subdivisions,
The sunsets pour blood and fire over you hundreds
and hundreds of nights, flat lands—blood and
fire of sunsets thousands of years have been
pouring over you.
And the stars follow the sunsets. One gold star. A
shower of blue stars. Blurs of white and grey
stars. Vast marching processions of stars arching
over you flat lands where frogs sob this April
night.
'Lots for Sale—Easy Terms' run letters painted on a
board—and the stars wheel onward, the frogs
sob this April night.

71. Joliet

ON the one hand the steel works.
On the other hand the penitentiary.
Sante Fé trains and Alton trains
Between smokestacks on the west
And grey walls on the east.
And Lockport down the river.

Part of the valley is God's,
And part is man's.
The river course laid out
A thousand years ago.
The canals ten years back.

The sun on two canals and one river
Makes three stripes of silver
Or copper and gold
Or shattered sunflower leaves.
Talons of an iceberg
Scraped out this valley.
Claws of an avalanche loosed here.

72. The Sea Hold

THE sea is large.
The sea hold on a leg of land in the Chesapeake
hugs an early sunset and a last morning star
over the oyster beds and the late clam boats of
lonely men.
Five white houses on a half-mile strip of land . . .
five white dice rolled from a tube.

Not so long ago . . . the sea was large . . .
And to-day the sea has lost nothing . . . it keeps all.

I am a loon about the sea.
I make so many sea songs, I cry so many sea cries, I
forget so many sea songs and sea cries.

I am a loon about the sea.
So are five men I had a fish fry with once in a tar-
paper shack trembling in a sand storm.
The sea knows more about them than they know
themselves.
They know only how the sea hugs and will not let go.

The sea is large.
The sea must know more than any of us.

73. Bricklayer Love

I THOUGHT of killing myself because I am only a bricklayer and you a woman who loves the man who runs a drug store.

I don't care like I used to; I lay bricks straighter than I used to and I sing slower handling the trowel afternoons.

When the sun is in my eyes and the ladders are shaky and the mortar boards go wrong, I think of you.

74.   Ashurnatsirpal III

(From Babylonian tablet, 4,000 *years Before Christ)*

THREE walls around the town of Tela when I
    came.
They expected everything of those walls;
Nobody in the town came out to kiss my feet.

I knocked the walls down, killed three thousand sol-
    diers,
Took away cattle and sheep, took all the loot in sight,
And burned special captives.

Some of the soldiers—I cut off hands and feet.
Others—I cut off ears and fingers.
Some—I put out the eyes.
I made a pyramid of heads.
I strung heads on trees circling the town.

When I got through with it
There wasn't much left of the town of Tela.

75. Mammy Hums

THIS is the song I rested with:
The right shoulder of a strong man I leaned on.
The face of the rain that drizzled on the short neck of
a canal boat.
The eyes of a child who slept while death went over
and under.
The petals of peony pink that fluttered in a shot of
wind come and gone.

This is the song I rested with:
Head, heels, and fingers rocked to the nigger mammy
humming of it, to the mile-off steamboat land-
ing whistle of it.

The murmurs run with bees' wings
in a late summer sun.
They go and come with white surf
slamming on a beach all day.

Get this.
And then you may sleep with a late afternoon slum-
ber sun.
Then you may slip your head in an elbow knowing
nothing—only sleep.

Mammy Hums

If so you sleep in the house of our song,
If so you sleep under the apple trees of our song,
Then the face of sleep must be the one face you were
    looking for.

76. Cool Tombs

WHEN Abraham Lincoln was shovelled into the tombs, he forgot the copperheads and the assassin . . . in the dust, in the cool tombs.

And Ulysses Grant lost all thought of con men and Wall Street, cash and collateral turned ashes . . . in the dust, in the cool tombs.

Pocahontas' body, lovely as a poplar, sweet as a red haw in November or a pawpaw in May, did she wonder? does she remember? . . . in the dust, in the cool tombs?

Take any streetful of people buying clothes and groceries, cheering a hero or throwing confetti and blowing tin horns . . . tell me if the lovers are losers . . . tell me if any get more than the lovers . . . in the dust . . . in the cool tombs.

77. Shenandoah

IN the Shenandoah Valley, one rider grey and one
rider blue, and the sun on the riders wondering.

Piled in the Shenandoah, riders blue and riders grey,
piled with shovels, one and another, dust in the
Shenandoah taking them quicker than mothers
take children done with play.
The blue nobody remembers, the grey nobody remem-
bers, it's all old and old nowadays in the Shenan-
doah.

.   .   ..

And all is young, a butter of dandelions slung on the
turf, climbing blue flowers of the wishing wood-
lands wondering: a midnight purple violet claims
the sun among old heads, among old dreams of
repeating heads of a rider blue and a rider grey
in the Shenandoah.

78. Grass

PILE the bodies high at Austerlitz and Waterloo.
  Shovel them under and let me work—
                    I am the grass; I cover all.

And pile them high at Gettysburg
And pile them high at Ypres and Verdun.
Shovel them under and let me work.
Two years, ten years, and passengers ask the con-
    ductor:
                    What place is this?
                    Where are we now?

                    I am the grass.
                    Let me work.

79. Old Timers

I AM an ancient reluctant conscript.

On the soup wagons of Xerxes I was a cleaner of
    pans.

On the march of Miltiades' phalanx I had a haft and
    head;
I had a bristling gleaming spear-handle.

Red-headed Cæsar picked me for a teamster.
He said, 'Go to work, you Tuscan bastard,
Rome calls for a man who can drive horses.'

The units of conquest led by Charles the Twelfth,
The whirling whimsical Napoleonic columns:
They saw me one of the horseshoers.

I trimmed the feet of a white horse Bonaparte swept
    the night stars with.
Lincoln said, 'Get into the game; your nation takes
    you.'
And I drove a wagon and team and I had my arm
    shot off
At Spotsylvania Court House.

I am an ancient reluctant conscript.

80. House

TWO Swede families live downstairs and an Irish policeman upstairs, and an old soldier, Uncle Joe.

Two Swede boys go upstairs and see Joe. His wife is dead, his only son is dead, and his two daughters in Missouri and Texas don't want him around.

The boys and Uncle Joe crack walnuts with a hammer on the bottom of a flatiron while the January wind howls and the zero air weaves laces on the window glass.

Joe tells the Swede boys all about Chickamauga and Chattanooga, how the Union soldiers crept in rain somewhere a dark night and ran forward and killed many Rebels, took flags, held a hill, and won a victory told about in the histories in school.

Joe takes a piece of carpenter's chalk, draws lines on the floor and piles stove wood to show where six regiments were slaughtered climbing a slope.

'Here they went' and 'Here they went,' says Joe, and the January wind howls and the zero air weaves laces on the window glass.

The two Swede boys go downstairs with a big blur of guns, men, and hills in their heads. They eat herring and potatoes and tell the family war is a wonder and soldiers are a wonder.

One breaks out with a cry at supper: I wish we had a war now and I could be a soldier.

81. Smoke and Steel

SMOKE of the fields in spring is one,
Smoke of the leaves in autumn another.
Smoke of a steel-mill roof or a battleship funnel,
They all go up in a line with a smokestack,
Or they twist . . . in the slow twist . . . of the
  wind.

If the north wind comes they run to the south.
If the west wind comes they run to the east.
   By this sign
   all smokes
   know each other.
Smoke of the fields in spring and leaves in autumn,
Smoke of the finished steel, chilled and blue,
By the oath of work they swear: 'I know you.'

Hunted and hissed from the centre
Deep down long ago when God made us over,
Deep down are the cinders we came from—
You and I and our heads of smoke.

 . . . .

Some of the smokes God dropped on the job
Cross on the sky and count our years
And sing in the secrets of our numbers;
Sing their dawns and sing their evenings,
Sing an old log-fire song:
   You may put the damper up,

Smoke and Steel

You may put the damper down,
The smoke goes up the chimney just the same.

Smoke of a city sunset skyline,
Smoke of a country dusk horizon—
They cross on the sky and count our years.

. . . .

Smoke of a brick-red dust
Winds on a spiral
Out of the stacks
For a hidden and glimpsing moon.
This, said the bar-iron shed to the blooming mill,
This is the slang of coal and steel.
The day-gang hands it to the night-gang,
The night-gang hands it back.

Stammer at the slang of this—
Let us understand half of it.
In the rolling mills and sheet mills,
In the harr and boom of the blast fires,
The smoke changes its shadow
And men change their shadow;
A nigger, a wop, a bohunk changes.

A bar of steel—it is only
Smoke at the heart of it, smoke and the blood of a man.
A runner of fire ran in it, ran out, ran somewhere else,
And left—smoke and the blood of a man
And the finished steel, chilled and blue.

Smoke and Steel

So fire runs in, runs out, runs somewhere else again,
And the bar of steel is a gun, a wheel, a nail, a shovel,
A rudder under the sea, a steering-gear in the sky;
And always dark in the heart and through it,
     Smoke and the blood of a man.
Pittsburg, Youngstown, Gary—they make their steel
    with men.
In the blood of men and the ink of chimneys
The smoke nights write their oaths:
Smoke into steel and blood into steel;
Homestead, Braddock, Birmingham, they make their
    steel with men.
Smoke and blood is the mix of steel.

    The birdmen drone
    in the blue; it is steel
    a motor sings and zooms.

   . . . .

Steel barb-wire around The Works.
Steel guns in the holsters of the guards at the gates of
    The Works.
Steel ore-boats bring the loads clawed from the earth
    by steel, lifted and lugged by arms of steel, sung on
    its way by the clanking clam-shells.
The runners now, the handlers now, are steel; they dig
    and clutch and haul; they hoist their automatic
    knuckles from job to job; they are steel making
    steel.

Smoke and Steel

Fire and dust and air fight in the furnaces; the pour is
    timed, the billets wriggle; the clinkers are dumped:
Liners on the sea, skyscrapers on the land; diving steel
    in the sea, climbing steel in the sky.

      . . . .

Finders in the dark, you Steve with a dinner bucket,
    you Steve clumping in the dusk on the sidewalks
    with an evening paper for the woman and kids,
    you Steve with your head wondering where we
    all end up—
Finders in the dark, Steve: I hook my arm in cinder
    sleeves; we go down the street together; it is all
    the same to us; you Steve and the rest of us end
    on the same stars; we all wear a hat in hell together,
    in hell or heaven.

    Smoke nights now, Steve.
    Smoke, smoke, lost in the sieves of yesterday;
    Dumped again to the scoops and hooks to-day.
    Smoke like the clocks and whistles, always.
        Smoke nights now.
        To-morrow something else.

      . . . .

Luck moons come and go;
Five men swim in a pot of red steel.
Their bones are kneaded into the bread of steel:
Their bones are knocked into coils and anvils
And the sucking plungers of sea-fighting turbines.
Look for them in the woven frame of a wireless station.

Smoke and Steel

So ghosts hide in steel like heavy-armed men in mirrors.
Peepers, skulkers—they shadow-dance in laughing tombs.
They are always there and they never answer.

One of them said: 'I like my job, the company is good
    to me, America is a wonderful country.'
One: 'Jesus, my bones ache; the company is a liar; this
    is a free country, like hell.'
  One: 'I got a girl, a peach; we save up and go on a
    farm and raise pigs and be the boss ourselves.'
And the others were roughneck singers a long ways from
    home.
Look for them back of a steel vault door.

      They laugh at the cost.
      They lift the birdmen into the blue.
      It is steel a motor sings and zooms.

In the subway plugs and drums,
In the slow hydraulic drills, in gumbo or gravel,
Under dynamo shafts in the webs of armature spiders,
They shadow-dance and laugh at the cost.

   .   .   .   .

The ovens light a red dome.
Spools of fire wind and wind.
Quadrangles of crimson sputter.
The lashes of dying maroon let down.
Fire and wind wash out the slag.
Forever the slag gets washed in fire and wind

Smoke and Steel

The anthem learned by the steel is:
>Do this or go hungry.
Look for our rust on a plough.
Listen to us in a threshing-engine razz.
Look at our job in the running wagon wheat.

. . . .

Fire and wind wash at the slag.
Box-cars, clocks, steam-shovels, churns, pistons, boilers, scissors—
Oh, the sleeping slag from the mountains, the slag-heavy pig-iron will go down many roads.
Men will stab and shoot with it, and make butter and tunnel rivers, and mow hay in swaths, and slit hogs and skin beeves, and steer airplanes across North America, Europe, Asia, round the world.

Hacked from a hard rock country, broken and baked in mills and smelters, the rusty dust waits
Till the clean hard weave of its atoms cripples and blunts the drills chewing a hole in it.
The steel of its plinths and flanges is reckoned, O God, in one-millionth of an inch.

. . . .

Once when I saw the curves of fire, the rough scarf women dancing,
Dancing out of the flues and smokestacks—flying hair of fire, flying feet upside down;
Buckets and baskets of fire exploding and chortling, fire running wild out of the steady and fastened ovens;

148

Smoke and Steel

Sparks cracking a harr-harr-huff from a solar-plexus of
    rock-ribs of the earth taking a laugh for them-
    selves;
Ears and noses of fire, gibbering gorilla arms of fire, gold
    mud-pies, gold bird-wings, red jackets riding pur-
    ple mules, scarlet autocrats tumbling from the
    humps of camels, assassinated czars straddling ver-
    milion balloons;
I saw then the fires flash one by one: good-bye: then
    smoke, smoke;
And in the screens the great sisters of night and cool
    stars, sitting women arranging their hair,
Waiting in the sky, waiting with slow easy eyes, waiting
    and half-murmuring:
        'Since you know all
        and I know nothing,
        tell me what I dreamed last night.'

   . . . .

Pearl cobwebs in the windy rain,
in only a flicker of wind,
are caught and lost and never known again.

A pool of moonshine comes and waits,
but never waits long: the wind picks up
loose gold like this and is gone.

A bar of steel sleeps and looks slant-eyed
on the pearl cobwebs, the pools of moonshine;
sleeps slant-eyed a million years,

sleeps with a coat of rust, a vest of moths,
a shirt of gathering sod and loam.

The wind never bothers . . . a bar of steel.
The wind picks only . . . pearl cobwebs . . . pools of
   moonshine.

82.   Five Towns on the B. and O.

BY day . . . tireless smokestacks . . . hungry
smoky shanties hanging to the slopes . . .
crooning: We get by, that's all.

By night . . . all lit up . . . fire-gold bars, fire-
gold flues . . . and the shanties shaking in
clumsy shadows . . . almost the hills shaking
. . . all crooning:

By God, we're going to find out or know why.

83. Work Gangs

BOX cars run by a mile long.
And I wonder what they say to each other
When they stop a mile long on a sidetrack.
    Maybe their chatter goes:
I came from Fargo with a load of wheat up to the
    danger line.
I came from Omaha with a load of shorthorns and
    they splintered my boards.
I came from Detroit heavy with a load of flivvers.
I carried apples from the Hood river last year and
    this year bunches of bananas from Florida; they
    look for me with watermelons from Mississippi
    next year.

Hammers and shovels of work gangs sleep in shop
    corners
when the dark stars come on the sky and the night
    watchmen walk and look.

Then the hammer heads talk to the handles,
then the scoops of the shovels talk,
how the day's work nicked and trimmed them,
how they swung and lifted all day,
how the hands of the work gangs smelled of hope.
In the night of the dark stars
when the curve of the sky is a work gang handle,

152

Work Gangs

in the night on the mile-long sidetracks,
in the night where the hammers and shovels sleep in
    corners,
the night watchmen stuff their pipes with dreams—
and sometimes they doze and don't care for nothin',
and sometimes they search their heads for meanings,
    stories, stars.
    The stuff of it runs like this:
A long way we come; a long way to go; long rests and
    long deep sniffs for our lungs on the way.
Sleep is a belonging of all; even if all songs are old
    songs and the singing heart is snuffed out like a
    switchman's lantern with the oil gone, even if we
    forget our names and houses in the finish, the se-
    cret of sleep is left us, sleep belongs to all, sleep is
    the first and last and best of all.

People singing; people with song mouths connecting
    with song hearts; people who must sing or die;
    people whose song hearts break if there is no song
    mouth; these are my people.

84. Pennsylvania

I HAVE been in Pennsylvania,
In the Monongahela and the Hocking Valleys.

In the blue Susquehanna
On a Saturday morning
I saw the mounted constabulary go by,
I saw boys playing marbles.
Spring and the hills laughed.

And in places
Along the Appalachian chain,
I saw steel arms handling coal and iron,
And I saw the white-cauliflower faces
Of miners' wives waiting for the men to come home
    from the day's work.

I made colour studies in crimson and violet
Over the dust and domes of culm at sunset.

85. Whirls

NEITHER rose leaves gathered in a jar—respectably in Boston—these—nor drops of Christ blood for a chalice—decently in Philadelphia or Baltimore.

Cinders—these—hissing in a marl and lime of Chicago—also these—the howling of north-west winds across North and South Dakota—or the spatter of winter spray on sea rocks of Kamchatka.

86. People Who Must

I PAINTED on the roof of a skyscraper.
I painted a long while and called it a day's work.
The people on a corner swarmed and the traffic cop's
   whistle never let up all afternoon.
They were the same as bugs, many bugs on their
   way—
Those people on the go or at a standstill;
And the traffic cop a spot of blue, a splinter of brass,
Where the black tides ran around him
And he kept the street. I painted a long while
And called it a day's work.

87. Alley Rats

THEY were calling certain styles of whiskers by the
name of 'lilacs.'
And another manner of beard assumed in their chatter
a verbal guise
Of 'mutton chops,' 'galways,' 'feather dusters.'

Metaphors such as these sprang from their lips while
other street cries
Sprang from sparrows finding scattered oats among
interstices of the curb.
Ah-hah these metaphors—and Ah-hah these boys—
among the police they were known
As the Dirty Dozen and their names took the front
pages of newspapers.
And two of them croaked on the same day at a 'neck-
tie party' . . . if we employ the metaphors of
their lips.

88. Eleventh Avenue Racket

THERE is something terrible
about a hurdy-gurdy,
a gipsy man and woman,
and a monkey in red flannel
all stopping in front of a big house
with a sign 'For Rent' on the door
and the blinds hanging loose
and nobody home.
I never saw this.
I hope to God I never will.

Whoop-de-doodle-de-doo.
Hoodle-de-harr-de-hum.
Nobody home? Everybody home.
Whoop-de-doodle-de-doo.
Mamie Riley married Jimmy Higgins last night: Eddie
Jones died of whooping cough: George Hacks got
a job on the police force: the Rosenheims bought
a brass bed: Lena Hart giggled at a jackie: a push-
cart man called to*may*toes, to*may*toes.
Whoop-de-doodle-de-doo.
Hoodle-de-harr-de-hum.
Nobody home? Everybody home.

89. Home Fires

IN a Yiddish eating place on Rivington Street . . .
faces . . . coffee spots . . . children kicking
at the night stars with bare toes from bare but-
tocks.

They know it is September on Rivington when the
red tomaytoes cram the pushcarts,

Here the children snozzle at milk bottles, children
who have never seen a cow.

Here the stranger wonders how so many people re-
member where they keep home fires.

90. Hats

HATS, where do you belong?
What is under you?

On the rim of a skyscraper's forehead
I looked down and saw: hats: fifty thousand hats:
Swarming with a noise of bees and sheep, cattle and
   waterfalls,
Stopping with a silence of sea grass, a silence of prairie
   corn.
          Hats: tell me your high hopes.

91. They All Want to Play Hamlet

THEY all want to play Hamlet.
    They have not exactly seen their fathers killed
Nor their mothers in a frame-up to kill,
Nor an Ophelia dying with a dust gagging the heart,
Not exactly the spinning circles of singing golden
        spiders,
Not exactly this have they got at nor the meaning of
        flowers—O flowers, flowers slung by a dancing
        girl—in the saddest play the inkfish, Shakespeare,
        ever wrote:
Yet they all want to play Hamlet because it is sad
        like all actors are sad and to stand by an open
        grave with a joker's skull in the hand and then
        to say over slow and say over slow wise, keen,
        beautiful words masking a heart that's break-
        ing, breaking.
This is something that calls and calls to their blood.
They are acting when they talk about it and they know
        it is acting to be particular about it and yet:
        They all want to play Hamlet.

92.   The Mayor of Gary

I ASKED the Mayor of Gary about the 12-hour day
and the 7-day week.

And the Mayor of Gary answered more workmen steal
time on the job in Gary than any other place in
the United States.

'Go into the plants and you will see men sitting around
doing nothing—machinery does everything,' said
the Mayor of Gary when I asked him about the
12-hour day and the 7-day week.

And he wore cool cream pants, the Mayor of Gary,
and white shoes, and a barber had fixed him up
with a shampoo and a shave and he was easy and
imperturbable though the government weather
bureau thermometer said 96 and children were
soaking their heads at bubbling fountains on the
street corners.

And I said good-bye to the Mayor of Gary and I went
out from the city hall and turned the corner into
Broadway.

And I saw workmen wearing leather shoes scruffed
with fire and cinders, and pitted with little holes
from running molten steel,

And some had bunches of specialized muscles around
their shoulder blades hard as pig iron, muscles of
their forearms were sheet steel and they looked to
me like men who had been somewhere.

Gary, Indiana, 1915.

93. Omaha

RED barns and red heifers spot the green
grass circles around Omaha—the farmers
haul tanks of cream and wagon loads of cheese.

Shale hogbacks across the river at Council
Bluffs—and shanties hang by an eyelash to
the hill slants back around Omaha.

A span of steel ties up the kin of Iowa and
Nebraska across the yellow, big-hoofed Missouri
River.

Omaha, the roughneck, feeds armies,
Eats and swears from a dirty face.
Omaha works to get the world a breakfast.

94. Real Estate News

ARMOUR AVENUE was the name of this street, and door signs on empty houses read 'The Silver Dollar,' 'Swede Annie' and the Christian names of madams such as 'Myrtle' and 'Jenny.'

Scrap iron, rags and bottles fill the front rooms hither and yon and signs in Yiddish say Abe Kaplan & Co. are running junk shops in whore-houses of former times.

The segregated district, the *Tenderloin*, is here no more; the red lights are gone; the ring of shovels handling scrap iron replaces the banging of pianos and the bawling songs of pimps.

Chicago, 1915.

95.   Manual System

MARY has a thingamajig clamped on her ears
And sits all day taking plugs out and sticking plugs
in.
Flashes and flashes—voices and voices
                    calling for ears to pour words in;
Faces at the ends of wires asking for other faces
                    at the ends of other wires:
All day taking plugs out and sticking plugs in,
Mary has a thingamajig clamped on her ears.

96. Honky Tonk in Cleveland, Ohio

IT'S a jazz affair, drum crashes and cornet razzes.
The trombone pony neighs and the tuba jackass snorts.
The banjo tickles and titters too awful.
The chippies talk about the funnies in the papers.
    The cartoonists weep in their beer.
    Ship riveters talk with their feet
    To the feet of floozies under the tables.
A quartet of white hopes mourn with interspersed
    snickers:
    'I got the blues.
    I got the blues.
    I got the blues.'
And . . . as we said earlier:
    The cartoonists weep in their beer.

97.   Crapshooters

SOMEBODY loses whenever somebody wins
This was known to the Chaldeans long ago
And more: somebody wins whenever somebody loses.
This too was in the savvy of the Chaldeans.

They take it heaven's hereafter is an eternity of crap
      games where they try their wrists years and years
      and no police come with a wagon; the game
      goes on for ever.
The spots on the dice are the music signs of the songs
      of heaven here.
God is Luck: Luck is God: we are all bones the High
      Thrower rolled: some are two spots, some double
      sixes.

The myths are Phoebe, Little Joe, Big Dick.
Hope runs high with a: Huh, seven—huh, come seven.
This too was in the savvy of the Chaldeans.

98. Boy and Father

THE boy Alexander understands his father to be a
    famous lawyer.
The leather law books of Alexander's father fill a
    room like hay in a barn.
Alexander has asked his father to let him build a
    house like bricklayers build, a house with walls
    and roofs made of big leather law books.

      The rain beats on the windows
      And the raindrops run down the window glass
      And the raindrops slide off the green blinds
        down the siding.
The boy Alexander dreams of Napoleon in John C.
    Abbott's history, Napoleon the grand and lonely
    man wronged, Napoleon in his life wronged and
    in his memory wronged.
The boy Alexander dreams of the cat Alice saw, the
    cat fading off into the dark and leaving the teeth
    of its Cheshire smile lighting the gloom.

Buffaloes, blizzards, way down in Texas, in the pan-
    handle of Texas snuggling close to New Mexico,
These creep into Alexander's dreaming by the win-
    dow when his father talks with strange men
    about land down in Deaf Smith County.

Boy and Father

Alexander's father tells the strange men: Five years ago
    we ran a Ford out on the prairie and chased ante-
    lopes.

Only once or twice in a long while has Alexander heard
    his father say 'my first wife' so-and-so and such-
    and-such.
A few times softly the father has told Alexander, 'Your
    mother . . . was a beautiful woman . . . but
    we won't talk about her.'
Always Alexander listens with a keen listen when he
    hears his father mention 'my first wife' or 'Alex-
    ander's mother.'

Alexander's father smokes a cigar and the Episcopal
    rector smokes a cigar, and the words come often:
    mystery of life, mystery of life.
These two come into Alexander's head blurry and grey
    while the rain beats on the windows and the rain-
    drops run down the window glass and the rain-
    drops slide off the green blinds and down the siding.
These and: There is a God, there must be a God, how
    can there be rain or sun unless there is a God?

So from the wrongs of Napoleon and the Cheshire cat
    smile on to the buffaloes and blizzards of Texas
    and on to his mother and to God, so the blurry grey

Boy and Father

rain dreams of Alexander have gone on five min-
utes, maybe ten, keeping slow easy time to the rain-
drops on the window glass and the raindrops sliding
off the green blinds and down the siding.

99. Clean Curtains

NEW neighbours came to the corner house at Congress and Green Streets.

The look of their clean white curtains was the same as the rim of a nun's bonnet.

One way was an oyster pail factory, one way they made candy, one way paper boxes, strawboard cartons.

The warehouse trucks shook the dust of the ways loose and the wheels whirled dust—there was dust of hoof and wagon wheel and rubber tyre—dust of police and fire wagons—dust of the winds that circled at midnights and noon listening to no prayers.

'O mother, I know the heart of you,' I sang passing the rim of a nun's bonnet—O white curtains—and people clean as the prayers of Jesus here in the faded ramshackle at Congress and Green.

Dust and the thundering trucks won—the barrages of the street wheels and the lawless wind took their way—was it five weeks or six the little mother, the new neighbours, battled and then took away the white prayers in the windows?

100. Neighbours

ON Forty First Street
near Eighth Avenue
a frame house wobbles.

If houses went on crutches
this house would be
one of the cripples.

A sign on the house:
Church of the Living God
And Rescue Home for Orphan Children.

From a Greek coffee house
Across the street
A cabalistic jargon
Jabbers back.
    And men at tables
    Spill Peloponnesian syllables
    And speak of shovels for street work.
    And the new embankments of the Erie Railroad
    At Painted Post, Horse's Head, Salamanca.

101. Cohoots

PLAY it across the table.
  What if we steal this city blind?
If they want anything let 'em nail it down.

Harness bulls, dicks, front office men,
And the high goats up on the bench,
Ain't they all in cahoots?
Ain't it fifty-fifty all down the line,
Petemen, dips, boosters, stick-ups and guns—
        what's to hinder?

        Go fifty-fifty.
If they nail you call in a mouthpiece.
Fix it, you gazump, you slant-head, fix it.
        Feed 'em. . . .

Nothin' ever sticks to my fingers, nah, nah,
        nothin' like that,
But there ain't no law we got to wear mittens—
        huh—is there?
Mittens, that's a good one—mittens!
There oughta be a law everybody wear mittens.

102. Blue Maroons

'YOU slut,' he flung at her.
  It was more than a hundred times
He had thrown it into her face
And by this time it meant nothing to her.
She said to herself upstairs sweeping,
'Clocks are to tell time with, pitchers
Hold milk, spoons dip out gravy, and a
Coffee pot keeps the respect of those
Who drink coffee—I am a woman whose
Husband gives her a kiss once for ten
Times he throws it in my face, "You slut."
If I go to a small town and him along
Or if I go to a big city and him along,
What of it? Am I better off?' She swept
The upstairs and came downstairs to fix
Dinner for the family.

103. The Hangman at Home

WHAT does the hangman think about
   When he goes home at night from work?
When he sits down with his wife and
Children for a cup of coffee and a
Plate of ham and eggs, do they ask
Him if it was a good day's work
And everything went well, or do they
Stay off some topics and talk about
The weather, base ball, politics
And the comic strips in the papers
And the movies? Do they look at his
Hands when he reaches for the coffee
Or the ham and eggs? If the little
Ones say, Daddy, play horse, here's
A rope—does he answer like a joke:
I seen enough rope for to-day?
Or does his face light up like a
Bonfire of joy and does he say:
It's a good and dandy world we live
In? And if a white face moon looks
In through a window where a baby girl
Sleeps and the moon gleams mix with
Baby ears and baby hair—the hangman—
How does he act then? It must be easy
For him. Anything is easy for a hangman,
I guess.

104. Man, the Man-Hunter

I SAW Man, the man-hunter,
Hunting with a torch in one hand
And a kerosene can in the other,
Hunting with guns, ropes, shackles.

I listened
    And the high cry rang,
The high cry of Man, the man-hunter:
We'll get you yet, you sbxyzch!

I listened later.
    The high cry rang:
Kill him! kill him! the sbxyzch!

In the morning the sun saw
Two butts of something, a smoking rump.
And a warning in charred wood:
                Well, we got him,
                the sbxyzch.

105. The Sins of Kalamazoo

THE sins of Kalamazoo are neither scarlet nor
crimson.
The sins of Kalamazoo are a convict grey, a dish-
water drab.
And the people who sin the sins of Kalamazoo are
neither scarlet nor crimson.
They run to drabs and greys—and some of them
sing they shall be washed whiter than snow—
and some: We should worry.

Yes, Kalamazoo is a spot on the map
And the passenger trains stop there
And the factory smokestacks smoke
And the grocery stores are open Saturday nights
And the streets are free for citizens who vote
And inhabitants counted in the census.
Saturday night is the big night.
    Listen with your ears on a Saturday night in
        Kalamazoo
    And say to yourself: I hear America, I hear,
        what do I hear?

Main street there runs through the middle of the town
And there is a dirty post-office
And a dirty city hall
And a dirty railroad station

The Sins of Kalamazoo

And the United States flag cries, cries the Stars and
  Stripes to the four winds on Lincoln's birthday and
  the Fourth of July.

Kalamazoo kisses a hand to something far off.
Kalamazoo calls to a long horizon, to a shivering silver
  angel, to a creeping mystic what-is-it.
'We're here because we're here,' is the song of Kala-
  mazoo.
'We don't know where we're going but we're on our
  way,' are the words.
There are hound dogs of bronze on the public square,
  hound dogs looking far beyond the public square.

Sweethearts there in Kalamazoo
Go to the general delivery window of the post-office
And speak their names and ask for letters
And ask again, 'Are you sure there is nothing for me?
I wish you'd look again—there must be a letter for
  me.'

And sweethearts go to the city hall
And tell their names and say, 'We want a licence.'
And they go to an instalment house and buy a bed on
  time and a clock,
And the children grow up asking each other, 'What can
  we do to kill time?'
They grow up and go to the railroad station and buy
  tickets for Texas, Pennsylvania, Alaska.

The Sins of Kalamazoo

'Kalamazoo is all right,' they say. 'But I want to see
    the world.'
And when they have looked the world over they come
    back saying it is all like Kalamazoo.

The trains come in from the east and hoot for the cross-
    ings,
And buzz away to the peach country and Chicago to
    the west;
Or they come from the west and shoot on to the Battle
    Creek breakfast bazaars
And the speedbug heavens of Detroit.

'I hear America, I hear, *what* do I hear?'
Said a loafer lagging along on the sidewalks of Kala-
    mazoo,
Lagging along and asking questions, reading signs.

Oh yes, there is a town named Kalamazoo,
A spot on the map where the trains hesitate.
I saw the sign of a five and ten cent store there
And the Standard Oil Company and the International
    Harvester
And a graveyard and a ball grounds
And a short order counter where a man can get a stack
    of wheats
And a pool hall where a rounder leered confidential like
    and said:
'Lookin' for a quiet game?'

The Sins of Kalamazoo

The loafer lagged along and asked,
'Do you make guitars here?
Do you make boxes the singing wood winds ask to sleep
    in?
Do you rig up strings the singing wood winds sift over
    and sing low?'
The answer: 'We manufacture musical instruments
    here.'

Here I saw churches with steeples like hatpins,
Undertaking rooms with sample coffins in the show win-
    dow
And signs everywhere satisfaction is guaranteed,
Shooting galleries where men kill imitation pigeons,
And there were doctors for the sick,
And lawyers for people waiting in jail,
And a dog catcher and a superintendent of streets,
And telephones, water-works, trolley cars,
And newspapers with a splatter of telegrams from sister
    cities of Kalamazoo the round world over.

And the loafer lagging along said:
Kalamazoo, you ain't in a class by yourself;
I seen you before in a lot of places.
If you are nuts America is nuts.
      And lagging along he said bitterly:
      Before I came to Kalamazoo I was silent.
      Now I am gabby, God help me, I am gabby.

The Sins of Kalamazoo

Kalamazoo, both of us will do a fadeaway.
I will be carried out feet first
And time and the rain will chew you to dust
And the winds blow you away.

And an old, old mother will lay a green moss cover on
    my bones
And a green moss cover on the stones of your post-office
    and city hall.

    Best of all
I have loved your kiddies playing run-sheep-run
And cutting their initials on the ball ground fence.
They knew every time I fooled them who was fooled
    and how.

    Best of all
I have loved the red gold smoke of your sunsets;
I have loved a moon with a ring around it
Floating over your public square;
I have loved the white dawn frost of early winter silver
And purple over your railroad tracks and lumber yards.

    The wishing heart of you I loved, Kalamazoo.
      I sang bye-lo, bye-lo to your dreams.
I sang bye-lo to your hopes and songs.

The Sins of Kalamazoo

I wished to God there were hound dogs of bronze on
    your public square,
Hound dogs with bronze paws looking to a long horizon
    with a shivering silver-angel,
    a creeping mystic what-is-it.

106. Broken-Face Gargoyles

ALL I can give you is broken-face gargoyles.
It is too early to sing and dance at funerals,
Though I can whisper to you I am looking for an
undertaker humming a lullaby and throwing his
feet in a swift and mystic buck-and-wing, now
you see it and now you don't.

Fish to swim a pool in your garden flashing a speckled
silver,
A basket of wine-saps filling your room with flame-
dark for your eyes and the tang of valley or-
chards for your nose,
Such a beautiful pail of fish, such a beautiful peck of
apples, I cannot bring you now.
It is too early and I am not footloose yet.

I shall come in the night when I come with a ham-
mer and saw.
I shall come near your window, where you look out
when your eyes open in the morning,
And there I shall slam together bird-houses and bird-
baths for wing-loose wrens and hummers to live
in, birds with yellow wing tips to blur and buzz
soft all summer,
So I shall make little fool homes with doors, always
open doors for all and each to run away when
they want to.

Broken-Face Gargoyles

I shall come just like that even though now it is early
    and I am not yet footloose,
Even though I am still looking for an undertaker with
    a raw, wind-bitten face and a dance in his feet.
I make a date with you (put it down) for six o'clock in
    the evening a thousand years from now.

All I can give you now is broken-face gargoyles.
All I can give you now is a double gorilla head with
    two fish mouths and four eagle eyes hooked on
    a street wall, spouting water and looking two
    ways to the ends of the street for the new peo-
    ple, the young strangers, coming, coming, al-
    ways coming.

        It is early.
        I shall yet be footloose.

107. Aprons of Silence

MANY things I might have said to-day
And I kept my mouth shut.
So many times I was asked
To come and say the same things
Everybody was saying, no end
To the yes-yes, yes-yes,
        me-too, me-too.

The aprons of silence covered me.
A wire and hatch held my tongue.
I spit nails into an abyss and listened.
I shut off the gabble of Jones, Johnson, Smith,
All whose names take pages in the city directory.

I fixed up a padded cell and lugged it around.
I locked myself in and nobody knew it.
Only the keeper and the kept in the hoosegow
Knew it—on the streets, in the post-office,
On the cars, into the railroad station
Where the caller was calling, 'All aboard,
All aboard for . . . Blaa-blaa . . . Blaa-blaa,
Blaa-blaa . . . and all points northwest . . . all
        aboard.'
Here I took along my own hoosegow
And did business with my own thoughts.
Do you see? It must be the aprons of silence.

108. Death Snips Proud Men

DEATH is stronger than all the governments because the governments are men and men die and then death laughs: Now you see 'em, now you don't.

Death is stronger than all proud men and so death snips proud men on the nose, throws a pair of dice and says: Read 'em and weep.

Death sends a radiogram every day: When I want you I'll drop in—and then one day he comes with a master-key and lets himself in and says: We'll go now.

Death is a nurse mother with big arms: 'Twon't hurt you at all; it's your time now; you just need a long sleep, child; what have you had anyhow better than sleep?

109. Good Night

MANY ways to spell good night.

Fireworks at a pier on the Fourth of July
    spell it with red wheels and yellow spokes.
They fizz in the air, touch the water and quit.
Rockets make a trajectory of gold-and-blue
    and then go out.

Railroad trains at night spell with a smokestack mush-
    rooming a white pillar.

Steamboats turn a curve in the Mississippi crying in
    a baritone that crosses lowland cottonfields to a
    razorback hill.
It is easy to spell good night.
                Many ways to spell good night.

110. Shirt

MY shirt is a token and symbol
more than a cover for sun and rain,
my shirt is a signal,
and a teller of souls.

I can take off my shirt and tear it,
and so make a ripping razzly noise,
and the people will say,
'Look at him tear his shirt.'

I can keep my shirt on.
I can stick around and sing like a little bird
and look 'em all in the eye and never be fazed.
     I can keep my shirt on.

111. Jazz Fantasia

DRUM on your drums, batter on your banjoes,
sob on the long cool winding saxophones.
Go to it, O jazzmen.

Sling your knuckles on the bottoms of the happy tin
pans, let your trombones ooze, and go husha-husha-
hush with the slippery sand-paper.

Moan like an autumn wind high in the lonesome tree-
tops, moan soft like you wanted somebody terrible,
cry like a racing car slipping away from a motor-cycle
cop, bang-bang! you jazzmen, bang all together
drums, traps, banjoes, horns, tin cans—make two
people fight on the top of a stairway and scratch each
other's eyes in a clinch tumbling down the stairs.

Can the rough stuff . . . now a Mississippi steam-
boat pushes up the night river with a hoo-hoo-hoo-oo
. . . and the green lanterns calling to the high soft
stars . . . a red moon rides on the humps of the low
river hills . . . go to it, O jazzmen.

112. Purple Martins

IF we were such and so, the same as these,
maybe we too would be slingers and sliders,
tumbling half over in the water mirrors,
tumbling half over at the horse heads of the sun,
tumbling our purple numbers.

Twirl on, you and your satin blue.
Be water birds, be air birds.
Be these purple tumblers you are.

    Dip and get away
From loops into slip-knots,
Write your own ciphers and figure eights.
It is your wooded island here in Lincoln park.
Everybody knows this belongs to you.

    Five fat geese
Eat grass on a sod bank
And never count your slinging ciphers,
                 your sliding figure eights.

A man on a green paint iron bench,
Slouches his feet and sniffs in a book,
And looks at you and your loops and slip-knots,
And looks at you and your sheaths of satin blue,
And slouches again and sniffs in the book,

Purple Martins

And mumbles: It is an idle and a doctrinaire exploit.
Go on tumbling half over in the water mirrors.
Go on tumbling half over at the horse heads of the sun.
Be water birds, be air birds.
Be these purple tumblers you are.

113. Mask

TO have your face left overnight
   Flung on a board by a crazy sculptor;
To have your face drop off a board
And fall to pieces on a floor
Lost among lumps all finger-marked
         —How now?

To be calm and level, placed high,
Looking among perfect women bathing
 And among bareheaded long-armed men,
Corner dreams of a crazy sculptor,
And then to fall, drop clean off the board,
Four o'clock in the morning and not a dog
Nor a policeman anywhere—

      Hoo hoo!
   had it been my laughing face
   maybe I would laugh with you,
   but my lover's face, the face I give
   women and the moon and the sea!

114.   Four Preludes on Play-
things of the Wind

'The past is a bucket of ashes.'

I

THE woman named To-morrow
   sits with a hairpin in her teeth
and takes her time
and does her hair the way she wants it
and fastens at last the last braid and coil
and puts the hairpin where it belongs
and turns and drawls: Well, what of it?
My grandmother, Yesterday, is gone.
What of it? Let the dead be dead.

II

The doors were cedar
and the panels strips of gold
and the girls were golden girls
and the panels read and the girls chanted:
        We are the greatest city,
        the greatest nation:
        nothing like us ever was.
The doors are twisted on broken hinges.
Sheets of rain swish through on the wind
        where the golden girls ran and the panels
        read:

193

Four Preludes on Playthings of the Wind

We are the greatest city,
the greatest nation:
nothing like us ever was.

III

It has happened before.
Strong men put up a city and got
a nation together,
And paid singers to sing and women
to warble: We are the greatest city,
the greatest nation:
nothing like us ever was.

And while the singers sang
and the strong men listened
and paid the singers well
and felt good about it all,
there were rats and lizards who listened
. . . and the only listeners left now
. . . are . . . the rats . . . and the lizards.

And there are black crows
crying, 'Caw, caw,'
bringing mud and sticks
building a nest
over the words carved
on the doors where the panels were cedar
and the strips on the panels were gold
and the golden girls came singing:

Four Preludes on Playthings of the Wind

> We are the greatest city,
> the greatest nation:
> nothing like us ever was.

The only singers now are crows crying, 'Caw, caw,'
And the sheets of rain whine in the wind and doorways.
And the only listeners now are . . . the rats . . . and
the lizards.

IV

> The feet of the rats
> scribble on the door sills;
> the hieroglyphs of the rat footprints
> chatter the pedigrees of the rats
> and babble of the blood
> and gabble of the breed
> of the grandfathers and the great-grandfathers
> of the rats

> And the wind shifts
> and the dust on a door sill shifts
> and even the writing of the rat footprints
> tells us nothing, nothing at all
> about the greatest city, the greatest nation
> where the strong men listened
> and the women warbled: Nothing like us ever
> was.

115.   Ossawatomie

I DON'T know how he came,
shambling, dark, and strong.

He stood in the city and told men:
My people are fools, my people are young and strong,
    my people must learn, my people are terrible
    workers and fighters.
Always he kept on asking: Where did that blood come
    from?

They said: You for the fool killer,
        you for the booby hatch
        and a necktie party.

They hauled him into jail.
They sneered at him and spit on him,
And he wrecked their jails,
Singing, 'God damn your jails,'
And when he was most in jail
Crummy among the crazy in the dark
Then he was most of all out of jail
Shambling, dark, and strong,
Always asking: Where did that blood come from?

They laid hands on him
And the fool killers had a laugh

Ossawatomie

And the necktie party was a go, by God.
They laid hands on him and he was a goner.
  They hammered him to pieces and he stood up.
 They buried him and he walked out of the grave, by God,
  Asking again: Where did that blood come from?

116. Long Guns

THEN came, Oscar, the time of the guns.
And there was no land for a man, no land for a
country,
Unless guns sprang up
And spoke their language.
The how of running the world was all in guns.

The law of a God keeping sea and land apart,
The law of a child sucking milk,
The law of stars held together,
They slept and worked in the heads of men
Making twenty-mile guns, sixty-mile guns,
Speaking their language
Of no land for a man, no land for a country
Unless . . . guns . . . unless . . . guns.

There was a child wanted the moon shot off the sky,
asking a long gun to get the moon,
to conquer the insults of the moon,
to conquer something, anything,
to put it over and win the day,
To show them the running of the world was all in
guns.
There was a child wanted the moon shot off the sky.
They dreamed . . . in the time of the guns . . .
of guns.

117. The Lawyers Know too Much

THE lawyers, Bob, know too much.
They are chums of the books of old John Marshall.
They know it all, what a dead hand wrote,
A stiff dead hand and its knuckles crumbling,
The bones of the fingers a thin white ash.
　　The lawyers know
　　a dead man's thoughts too well.

In the heels of the higgling lawyers, Bob,
Too many slippery ifs and buts and howevers,
Too much hereinbefore provided whereas,
Too many doors to go in and out of.

　　When the lawyers are through
　　What is there left, Bob?
　　Can a mouse nibble at it
　　And find enough to fasten a tooth in?

　　Why is there always a secret singing
　　When a lawyer cashes in?
　　Why does a hearse horse snicker
　　Hauling a lawyer away?

The work of a bricklayer goes to the blue.
The knack of a mason outlasts a moon.

The Lawyers Know too Much

The hands of a plasterer hold a room together.
The land of a farmer wishes him back again.
    Singers of songs and dreamers of plays
    Build a house no wind blows over.
The lawyers—tell me why a hearse horse snickers haul-
    ing a lawyer's bones.

118. Losers

IF I should pass the tomb of Jonah
I would stop there and sit for awhile;
Because I was swallowed one time deep in the dark
And came out alive after all.

If I pass the burial spot of Nero
I shall say to the wind, 'Well, well!'—
I who have fiddled in a world on fire,
I who have done so many stunts not worth doing.

I am looking for the grave of Sindbad too.
I want to shake his ghost-hand and say,
'Neither of us died very early, did we?'

And the last sleeping-place of Nebuchadnezzar—
When I arrive there I shall tell the wind:
'You ate grass; I have eaten crow—
Who is better off now or next year?'

Jack Cade, John Brown, Jesse James,
There too I could sit down and stop for awhile.
I think I could tell their headstones:
'God, let us remember all good losers.'

Losers

I could ask people to throw ashes on their heads
In the name of that sergeant at Belleau Woods,
Walking into the drumfires, calling his men,
'Come on, you . . . Do you want to live for ever?'

119.   Threes

IWAS a boy when I heard three red words
a thousand Frenchmen died in the streets
for: Liberty, Equality, Fraternity—I asked
why men die for words.

I was older; men with moustaches, sideburns,
lilacs, told me the high golden words are:
Mother, Home, and Heaven—other older men with
face decorations said: God, Duty, Immortality
—they sang these threes slow from deep lungs.

Years ticked off their say-so on the great clocks
of doom and damnation, soup and nuts: meteors flashed
their say-so: and out of great Russia came three
dusky syllables workmen took guns and went out to die
for: Bread, Peace, Land.

And I met a marine of the U. S. A., a leatherneck
with a girl on his knee for a memory in ports circling
the earth and he said: Tell me how to say three things
and I always get by—gimme a plate of ham and eggs
—how much?—and—do you love me, kid?

120. Bas-Relief

FIVE geese deploy mysteriously.
  Onward proudly with flagstaffs,
Hearses with silver bugles,
Bushels of plum-blossoms dropping
For ten mystic web-feet—
Each his own drum-major,
Each charged with the honour
Of the ancient goose nation,
Each with a nose-length surpassing
The nose-lengths of rival nations,
Sombrely, slowly, unimpeachably,
Five geese deploy mysteriously.

121. Killers

I AM put high over all others in the city to-day.
I am the killer who kills for those who wish a killing
to-day.

Here is a strong young man who killed.
There was a driving wind of city dust and horse dung
blowing and he stood at an intersection of five
sewers and there pumped the bullets of an auto-
matic pistol into another man, a fellow-citizen.
Therefore, the prosecuting attorneys, fellow-citizens,
and a jury of his peers, also fellow-citizens, lis-
tened to the testimony of other fellow-citizens,
policemen, doctors, and after a verdict of guilty,
the judge, a fellow-citizen, said: I sentence you
to be hanged by the neck till you are dead.

So there is a killer to be killed and I am the killer of
the killer for to-day.
I don't know why it beats in my head in the lines I
read once in an old school reader: I'm to be queen
of the May, mother, I'm to be queen of the May.
Anyhow it comes back in language just like that to-day.

I am the high honourable killer to-day.
There are five million people in the State, five million
killers for whom I kill.
I am the killer who kills to-day for five million killers
who wish a killing.

122. Three Ghosts

THREE tailors of Tooley Street wrote: We, the
People.
The names are forgotten. It is a joke in ghosts.

Cutters or bushelmen or armhole basters, they sat
cross-legged stitching, snatched at scissors, stole each
other's thimbles.

Cross-legged, working for wages, joking each other
as misfits cut from the cloth of a Master Tailor,
they sat and spoke their thoughts of the glory of
The People, they met after work and drank beer to
The People.

Faded off into the twilights the names are forgotten.
It is a joke in ghosts. Let it ride. They wrote: We,
The People.

123. Jug

THE shale and water thrown together so-so first of all,

Then a potter's hand on the wheel and his fingers shaping the jug; out of the mud a mouth and a handle;

Slimpsy, loose and ready to fall at a touch, fire plays on it, slow fire coaxing all the water out of the shale mix.

Dipped in glaze more fire plays on it till a molasses lava runs in waves, rises and retreats, a varnish of volcanoes.

Take it now; out of mud now here is a mouth and handle; out of this now mothers will pour milk and maple syrup and cider, vinegar, apple juice, and sorghum.

There is nothing proud about this; only one out of many; the potter's wheel slings them out and the fires harden them hours and hours thousands and thousands.

'Be good to me, put me down easy on the floors of the new concrete houses; I was poured out like a concrete house and baked in fire too.'

124. Hoodlums

I AM a hoodlum, you are a hoodlum, we and all of
us are a world of hoodlums—maybe so.

I hate and kill better men than I am, so do you, so
do all of us—maybe—maybe so.

In the ends of my fingers the itch for another man's
neck, I want to see him hanging, one of dusk's
cartoons against the sunset.

This is the hate my father gave me, this was in my
mother's milk, this is you and me and all of us
in a world of hoodlums—maybe so.

Let us go on, brother hoodlums, let us kill and kill, it
has always been so, it will always be so, there is
nothing more to it.

Let us go on, sister hoodlums, kill, kill, and kill, the
torsos of the world's mothers are tireless and
the loins of the world's fathers are strong—so
go on—kill, kill, kill.

Lay them deep in the dirt, the stiffs we fixed, the
cadavers bumped off, lay them deep and let the
night winds of winter blizzards howl their burial
service.

The night winds and the winter, the great white sheets
of northern blizzards, who can sing better for
the lost hoodlums the old requiem, 'Kill him!
kill him! . . .'

Hoodlums

To-day my son, to-morrow yours, the day after your
next door neighbour's—it is all in the wrists of the
gods who shoot craps—it is anybody's guess whose
eyes shut next.

Being a hoodlum now, you and I, being all of us a
world of hoodlums, let us take up the cry when the
mob sluffs by on a thousand shoe soles, let us too
yammer, 'Kill him! kill him! . . .'

Let us do this now . . . for our mothers . . . for our
sisters and wives . . . let us kill, kill, kill—for
the torsos of the women are tireless and the loins
of the men are strong.

Chicago, July 29, 1919.

125. Slippery

THE six-month child
Fresh from the tub
Wriggles in our hands.
This is our fish child.
Give her a nickname: Slippery.

126. Baby Toes

THERE is a blue star, Janet,
  Fifteen years' ride from us,
If we ride a hundred miles an hour.

There is a white star, Janet,
Forty years' ride from us,
If we ride a hundred miles an hour.

Shall we ride
To the blue star
Or the white star?

127. Sleepyheads

SLEEP is a maker of makers. Birds sleep. Feet cling to a perch. Look at the balance. Let the legs loosen, the backbone untwist, the head go heavy over, the whole works tumbles a done bird off the perch.

Fox cubs sleep. The pointed head curls round into hind legs and tail. It is a ball of red hair. It is a muff waiting. A wind might whisk it in the air across pastures and rivers, a cocoon, a pod of seeds. The snooze of the black nose is in a circle of red hair.

Old men sleep. In chimney corners, in rocking chairs, at wood stoves, steam radiators. They talk and forget and nod and are out of talk with closed eyes. Forgetting to live. Knowing the time has come useless for them to live. Old eagles and old dogs run and fly in the dreams.

Babies sleep. In flannels the papoose faces, the bambino noses, and dodo, dodo the song of many matushkas. Babies—a leaf on a tree in the spring sun. A nub of a new thing sucks the sap of a tree in the sun, yes a new thing, a what-is-it? A left hand stirs, an eyelid twitches, the milk in the belly bubbles and gets to be blood and a left hand and an eyelid. Sleep is a maker of makers.

128. Half Moon in a High Wind

MONEY is nothing now, even if I had it,
O moony moon, yellow half moon,
Up over the green pines and grey elms,
Up in the new blue.

Streel, streel,
White lacey mist sheets of cloud,
Streel in the blowing of the wind,
Streel over the blue-and-moon sky,
Yellow gold half moon. It is light
On the snow; it is dark on the snow,
Streel, O lacey thin sheets, up in the new blue.

Come down, stay there, move on.
I want you, I don't, keep all.
There is no song to your singing.
I am hit deep, you drive far,
O moony yellow half moon,
Steady, steady, or will you tip over?
Or will the wind and the streeling
Thin sheets only pass and move on
And leave you alone and lovely?
I want you, I don't, come down,
Stay there, move on.
Money is nothing now, even if I had it.

129. Remorse

THE horse's name was Remorse.
  There were people said, 'Gee, what a nag!'
And they were Edgar Allan Poe bugs and so
They called him Remorse.
                              When he was a gelding
He flashed his heels to other ponies
And threw dust in the noses of other ponies
And won his first race and his second
And another and another and hardly ever
Came under the wire behind the other runners.

And so, Remorse, who is gone, was the hero of a play
By Henry Blossom, who is now gone.

What is there to a monicker? Call me anything.
A nut, a cheese, something that the cat brought in.
     Nick me with any old name.
Class me up for a fish, a gorilla, a slant head, an egg,
     a ham.
Only . . . slam me across the ears sometimes . . .
     and hunt for a white star
In my forehead and twist the bang of my forelock
     around it.
Make a wish for me. Maybe I will light out like a
     streak of wind.

130. Laughing Blue Steel

TWO fishes swimming in the sea,
  Two birds flying in the air,
Two chisels on an anvil—maybe.
Beaten, hammered, laughing blue steel to each other
      —maybe.
Sure I would rather be a chisel with you
                    than a fish.
Sure I would rather be a chisel with you
                    than a bird.
Take these two chisel-pals, O God.
Take 'em and beat 'em, hammer 'em,
                  hear 'em laugh.

131. Sandhill People

I TOOK away three pictures.
One was a white gull forming a half-mile arch
from the pines toward Waukegan.
One was a whistle in the little sandhills, a bird crying
either to the sunset gone or the dusk come.
One was three spotted waterbirds, zigzagging, cutting
scrolls and jags, writing a bird Sanscrit of wing
points, half over the sand, half over the water,
a half-love for the sea, a half-love for the land.

I took away three thoughts.
One was a thing my people call 'love,' a shut-in river
hunting the sea, breaking white falls between
tall clefs of hill country.
One was a thing my people call 'silence,' the wind
running over the butter-faced sand-flowers, run-
ning over the sea, and never heard of again.
One was a thing my people call 'death,' neither a
whistle in the little sandhills, nor a bird Sanscrit
of wing points, yet a coat all the stars and seas
have worn, yet a face the beach wears between
sunset and dusk.

132.   Accomplished Facts

EVERY year Emily Dickinson sent one friend
the first arbutus bud in the garden.

In a last will and testament Andrew Jackson
remembered a friend with the gift of George
Washington's pocket spy-glass.

Napoleon, too, in a last testament, mentioned a silver
watch taken from the bedroom of Frederick the Great,
and passed along this trophy to a particular friend.

O. Henry took a blood carnation from his coat lapel
and handed it to a country girl starting work in a
bean bazaar, and scribbled: 'Peach blossoms may or
may not stay pink in city dust.'

So it goes. Some things we buy, some not.
Tom Jefferson was proud of his radishes, and Abe
Lincoln blacked his own boots, and Bismarck called
Berlin a wilderness of brick and newspapers.

So it goes. There are accomplished facts.
Ride, ride, ride on in the great new blimps—
Cross unheard-of oceans, circle the planet.

Accomplished Facts

When you come back we may sit by five hollyhocks.
We might listen to boys fighting for marbles.
The grasshopper will look good to us.

So it goes . . .

133. Trinity Peace

THE grave of Alexander Hamilton is in Trinity yard at the end of Wall Street.

The grave of Robert Fulton likewise is in Trinity yard where Wall Street stops.

And in this yard stenogs, bundle boys, scrubwomen, sit on the tombstones, and walk on the grass of graves, speaking of war and weather, of babies, wages and love.

An iron picket fence . . . and streaming thousands along Broadway sidewalks . . . straw hats, faces, legs . . . a singing, talking, hustling river . . . down the great street that ends with a Sea.

. . . easy is the sleep of Alexander Hamilton.
. . . easy is the sleep of Robert Fulton.
. . . easy are the great governments and the great steamboats.

134. Portrait

(For S. A.)

TO write one book in five years
　　or five books in one year,
to be the painter and the thing painted,
. . . where are we, bo?

Wait—get his number.
The barber shop handling is here
and the tweeds, the cheviot, the Scotch Mist,
and the flame orange scarf.

Yet there is more—he sleeps under bridges
with lonely crazy men; he sits in country
jails with bootleggers; he adopts the children
of broken-down burlesque actresses; he has
cried a heart of tears for Windy MacPherson's
father; he pencils wrists of lonely women.

Can a man sit at a desk in a skyscraper in Chicago
and be a harness-maker in a corn town in Iowa
and feel the tall grass coming up in June
and the ache of the cottonwood trees
singing with the prairie wind?

135. Cups of Coffee

THE haggard woman with a hacking cough and a deathless love whispers of white flowers . . . in your poem you pour this like a cup of coffee, Gabriel.

The slim girl whose voice was lost in the waves of flesh piled on her bones . . . and the woman who sold to many men and saw her breasts shrivel . . . in two poems you pour these like a cup of coffee, François.

The woman whose lips are a thread of scarlet, the woman whose feet take hold on hell, the woman who turned to a memorial of salt looking at the lights of a forgotten city . . . in your affidavits, ancient Jews, you pour these like cups of coffee.

The woman who took men as snakes take rabbits, a rag and a bone and a hank of hair, she whose eyes called men to sea dreams and shark's teeth . . . in a poem you pour this like a cup of coffee, Kip.

Marching to the footlights in night robes with spots of blood, marching in white sheets muffling the

Cups of Coffee

faces, marching with heads in the air they come
back and cough and cry and sneer: . . . in
your poems, men, you pour these like cups of
coffee.

136.   Night Movement–New York

IN the night, when the sea-winds take the city in their
    arms,
And cool the loud streets that kept their dust noon
    and afternoon;
In the night, when the sea-birds call to the lights of
    the city,
The lights that cut on the skyline their name of a
    city;
In the night, when the trains and wagons start from
    a long way off
For the city where the people ask bread and want
    letters;
In the night the city lives too—the day is not all.
In the night there are dancers dancing and singers
    singing,
And the sailors and soldiers look for numbers on
    doors.
In the night the sea-winds take the city in their arms.

137.   Streets Too Old

I WALKED among the streets of an old city and the
streets were lean as the throats of hard seafish
soaked in salt and kept in barrels many years.

How old, how old, how old, we are:—the walls went
on saying, street walls leaning toward each other
like old women of the people, like old midwives
tired and only doing what must be done.

The greatest the city could offer me, a stranger, was
statues of the kings, on all corners bronzes of
kings—ancient bearded kings who wrote books
and spoke of God's love for all people—and
young kings who took forth armies out across
the frontiers splitting the heads of their oppo-
nents and enlarging their kingdoms.

Strangest of all to me, a stranger in this old city, was
the murmur always whistling on the winds twist-
ing out of the armpits and fingertips of the kings
in bronze:—Is there no loosening? Is this for
always?

In an early snow-flurry one cried:—Pull me down
where the tired old midwives no longer look at
me, throw the bronze of me to a fierce fire and
make me into neckchains for dancing children.

224

138. Mohammed ben Hadjet-lache

THIS Mohammedan colonel from the Caucasus yells
with his voice and wigwags with his arms.

The interpreter translates, 'I was a friend of Korni-
lov, he asks me what to do and I tell him.'

A stub of a man, this Mohammedan colonel . . . a
projectile shape . . . a bald head hammered . . .

'Does he fight or do they put him in a cannon and
shoot him at the enemy?'

This fly-by-night, this bull-roarer who knows every-
body.

'I write forty books, history of Islam, history of Eu-
rope, true religion, scientific farming, I am the
Roosevelt of the Caucasus, I go to America and
ride horses in the moving pictures for $500,000,
you get $50,000 . . .'

'I have 30,000 acres in the Caucasus, I have a stove
factory in Petrograd the Bolsheviks take from
me, I am an old friend of the Czar, I am an
old family friend of Clemenceau . . .'

These hands strangled three fellow-workers for the
Czarist restoration, took their money, sent them
in sacks to a river bottom . . . and scandalized
Stockholm with his gang of strangler women.

Mohammed ben Hadjetlache

Mid-sea strangler hands rise before me illustrating a
    wish, 'I ride horses for the moving pictures
    in America, $500,000, and you get ten per
    cent . . .'
This rider of fugitive dawns. . . .

139. Baltic Fog Notes

(Bergen)

SEVEN days all fog, all mist, and the turbines pounding through high seas.

I was a plaything, a rat's neck in the teeth of a scuffling mastiff.

Fog and fog and no stars, sun, moon.

Then an afternoon in fjords, low-lying lands scrawled in granite languages on a grey sky,

A night harbour, blue dusk mountain shoulders against a night sky,

And a circle of lights blinking: Ninety thousand people here.

> Among the Wednesday night thousands in goloshes and coats slickered for rain,
>
> I learned how hungry I was for streets and people.

. . . .

I would rather be water than anything else.

I saw a drive of salt fog and mist in the North Atlantic and an iceberg dusky as a cloud in the grey of morning.

And I saw the dream pools of fjords in Norway . . . and the scarf of dancing water on the rocks and over the edges of mountain shelves.

. . . .

Bury me in a mountain graveyard in Norway.

Baltic Fog Notes

Three tongues of water sing around it with snow from
the mountains.

Bury me in the North Atlantic.
A fog there from Iceland will be a murmur in grey
over me and a long deep wind sob always.

Bury me in an Illinois cornfield.
The blizzards loosen their pipe organ voluntaries in
winter stubble and the spring rains and the fall
rains bring letters from the sea.

140. Circles of Doors

I LOVE him, I love him, ran the patter of her lips
And she formed his name on her tongue and sang.
And she sent him word she loved him so much,
So much, and death was nothing; work, art, home,
All was nothing if her love for him was not first
Of all; the patter of her lips ran, I love him,
I love him; and he knew the doors that opened
Into doors and more doors, no end of doors,
And full length mirrors doubling and tripling
The apparitions of doors: circling corridors of
Looking glasses and doors, some with knobs, some
With no knobs, some opening slow to a heavy push,
And some jumping open at a touch and a hello.
And he knew if he so wished he could follow her
Swift running through circles of doors, hearing
Sometimes her whisper, I love him, I love him,
And sometimes only a high chaser of laughter
Somewhere five or ten doors ahead or five or ten
Doors behind, or chittering *h-st, h-st,* among corners
Of the tall full-length dusty looking glasses.
I love, I love, I love, she sang short and quick in
High thin beaten soprano and he knew the meanings,
The high chaser of laughter, the doors on doors
And the looking glasses, the room to room hunt,
The ends opening into new ends always.

141.   Two Strangers Breakfast

THE law says you and I belong to each other,
   George.
The law says you are mine and I am yours, George.
And there are a million miles of white snowstorms, a
   million furnaces of hell,
Between the chair where you sit and the chair where
   I sit.
The law says two strangers shall eat breakfast to-
   gether after nights on the horn of an Arctic
   moon.

142. Curse of a Rich Polish Peasant on his Sister who Ran Away with a Wild Man

FELIKSOWA has gone again from our house and this time for good, I hope.

She and her husband took with them the cow father gave them, and they sold it.

She went like a swine, because she called neither on me, her brother, nor on her father, before leaving for those forests.

That is where she ought to live, with bears, not with men.

She was something of an ape before and there, with her wild husband, she became altogether an ape.

No honest person would have done as they did.

Whose fault is it? And how much they have cursed me and their father!

May God not punish them for it. They think only about money; they let the church go if they can only live fat on their money.

143. An Electric Sign goes Dark

POLAND, France, Judea ran in her veins,
   Singing to Paris for bread, singing to Gotham in
   a fizz at the pop of a bottle's cork.

'Won't you come and play wiz me,' she sang . . .
   and 'I just can't make my eyes behave.'
'Higgeldy-Piggeldy,' 'Papa's Wife,' 'Follow Me'
   were plays.

Did she wash her feet in a tub of milk? Was a strand
   of pearls sneaked from her trunk? the news-
   papers asked.
Cigarettes, tulips, pacing horses, took her name.

Twenty years old . . . thirty . . . forty . . .
Forty-five and the doctors fathom nothing, the doc-
   tors quarrel, the doctors use silver tubes feeding
   twenty-four quarts of blood into the veins, the
   respects of a prize-fighter, a cab driver.
And a little mouth moans: It is easy to die when they
   are dying so many grand deaths in France.

A voice, a shape, gone.
A baby bundle from Warsaw . . . legs, torso, head
   . . . on a hotel bed at The Savoy.

An Electric Sign Goes Dark

The white chisellings of flesh that flung themselves in
    somersaults, straddles, for packed houses:
A memory, a stage and footlights out, an electric sign
    on Broadway dark.

She belonged to somebody, nobody.
No one man owned her, no ten nor a thousand.
She belonged to many thousand men, lovers of the white
    chiselling of arms and shoulders, the ivory of a
    laugh, the bells of song.

Railroad brakemen taking trains across Nebraska prairies,
    lumbermen jaunting in pine and tamarack of the
    North-West, stock-ranchers in the Middle West,
    mayors of southern cities
Say to their pals and wives now: I see by the papers
    Anna Held is dead.

144. Then Buy with an Eye to Looks

THE fine cloth of your love might be a fabric of
   Egypt
Something Sindbad, the sailor, took away from rob-
   bers,
Something a traveller with plenty of money might
   pick up
And bring home and stick on the walls and say:
'There's a little thing made a hit with me
When I was in Cairo—I think I must see Cairo
   again some day.'
So there are cornice manufacturers, chewing gum
   kings,
Young Napoleons who corner eggs or corner cheese,
Phenoms looking for more worlds to corner,
And still other phenoms who lard themselves in
And make a killing in steel, copper, permanganese,
And they say to random friends in for a call:
   'Have you had a look at my wife? Here she is.
   Haven't I got her dolled up for fair?'
O-ee! the fine cloth of your love might be a fabric
   of Egypt.

145. Proud and Beautiful

AFTER you have spent all the money modistes and
manicures and mannikins will take for fixing
you over into a thing the people on the streets
call proud and beautiful,

After the shops and fingers have worn out all they
have and know and can hope to have and know
for the sake of making you what the people on
the streets call proud and beautiful,

After there is absolutely nothing more to be done for
the sake of staging you as a great enigmatic bird
of paradise and they must all declare you to be
proud and beautiful,

After you have become the last word in good looks,
in so far as good looks may be fixed and formu-
lated, then, why then, there is nothing more to
it then, it is then you listen and see how voices
and eyes declare you to be proud and beautiful.

146. Put Off the Wedding Five Times and Nobody Comes to it

(Handbook for Quarrelling Lovers)

I THOUGHT of offering you apothegms.
I might have said, 'Dogs bark and the wind carries it away.'
I might have said, 'He who would make a door of gold must knock a nail in every day.'
So easy, so easy it would have been to inaugurate a high impetuous moment for you to look on before the final farewells were spoken.
You who assumed the farewells in the manner of people buying newspapers and reading the headlines—and all pedlars of gossip who buttonhole each other and wag their heads saying, 'Yes, I heard all about it last Wednesday.'

I considered several apothegms.
'There is no love but service,' of course, would only initiate a quarrel over who has served and how and when.
'Love stands against fire and flood and much bitterness,' would only initiate a second misunderstanding, and bickerings with lapses of silence.

236

Put Off the Wedding Five Times

What is there in the Bible to cover our case, or Shake-
    speare? What poetry can help? Is there any left
    but Epictetus?
Since you have already chosen to interpret silence for
    language and silence for despair and silence for
    contempt and silence for all things but love,
Since you have already chosen to read ashes where God
    knows there was something else than ashes,
Since silence and ashes are two identical findings for
    your eyes and there are no apothegms worth hand-
    ing out like a hung jury's verdict for a record in
    our own hearts as well as the community at large,
I can only remember a Russian peasant who told me
    his grandfather warned him: If you ride too good
    a horse you will not take the straight road to town.

It will always come back to me in the blur of that
    hokku: The heart of a woman of thirty is like the
    red ball of the sun seen through a mist.
Or I will remember the witchery in the eyes of a girl
    at a barn dance one winter night in Illinois saying:
        Put off the wedding five times and nobody
        comes to it.

147. Baby Vamps

BABY vamps, is it harder work than it used to be?
Are the new soda parlours worse than the old-time
saloons?
Baby vamps, do you have jobs in the day-time
or is this all you do?
do you come out only at night?
In the winter at the skating rinks, in the summer at
the roller coaster parks,
Wherever figure eights are carved, by skates in win-
ter, by roller coasters in summer,
Wherever the whirligigs are going and chicken span-
ish and hot dog are sold,
There you come, giggling baby vamp, there you come
with your blue baby eyes, saying:
Take me along.

148. Vaudeville Dancer

ELSIE FLIMMERWON, you got a job now with a jazz outfit in vaudeville.

The houses go wild when you finish the act shimmying a fast shimmy to The Livery Stable Blues.

It is long ago, Elsie Flimmerwon, I saw your mother over a washtub in a grape arbour when your father came with the locomotor ataxia shuffle.

It is long ago, Elsie, and now they spell your name with an electric sign.

Then you were a little thing in checked gingham and your mother wiped your nose and said: You little fool, keep off the streets.

Now you are a big girl at last and streetfuls of people read your name and a line of people shaped like a letter S stand at the box office hoping to see you shimmy.

149. Balloon Faces

THE balloons hang on wires in the Marigold Gardens.

They spot their yellow and gold, they juggle their blue and red, they float their faces on the face of the sky.

Balloon face eaters sit by hundreds reading the eat cards, asking, 'What shall we eat?'—and the waiters, 'Have you ordered?' they are sixty balloon faces sifting white over the tuxedoes.

Poets, lawyers, ad men, mason contractors, smart-alecks discussing 'educated jackasses,' here they put crabs into their balloon faces.

Here sit the heavy balloon face women lifting crimson lobsters into their crimson faces, lobsters out of Sargasso sea bottoms.

Here sits a man cross-examining a woman, 'Where were you last night? What do you do with all your money? Who's buying your shoes now, anyhow?'

So they sit eating whitefish, two balloon faces swept on God's night wind.

And all the time the balloon spots on the wires, a little mile of festoons, they play their own silence play of film yellow and film gold, bubble blue and bubble red.

The wind crosses the town, the wind from the west side comes to the banks of marigolds boxed in the Marigold Gardens.

Balloon Faces

Night moths fly and fix their feet in the leaves and eat
and are seen by the eaters.

The jazz outfit sweats and the drums and the saxophones
reach for the ears of the eaters.

The chorus brought from Broadway works at the fun
and the slouch of their shoulders, the kick of their
ankles, reach for the eyes of the eaters.

These girls from Kokomo and Peoria, these hungry
girls, since they are paid-for, let us look on and
listen, let us get their number.

Why do I go again to the balloons on the wires, some-
thing for nothing, kin women of the half-moon,
dream women?

And the half-moon swinging on the wind crossing the
town—these two, the half-moon and the wind—
this will be about all, this will be about all.

Eaters, go to it; your mazuma pays for it all; it's a
knockout, a classy knockout—and pay day always
comes.

The moths in the marigolds will do for me, the half-
moon, the wishing wind and the little mile of bal-
loon spots on wires—this will be about all, this will
be about all.

150.   Haze

KEEP a red heart of memories
  Under the great grey rain sheds of the sky,
  Under the open sun and the yellow gloaming embers.
  Remember all pay days of lilacs and songbirds;
  All starlights of cool memories on storm paths.

Out of this prairie rise the faces of dead men.
They speak to me. I cannot tell you what they say.

Other faces rise on the prairie.
                  They are the unborn. The future.

Yesterday and to-morrow cross and mix on the sky-
    line
The two are lost in a purple haze. One forgets. One
    waits.

In the yellow dust of sunsets, in the meadows of ver-
    milion eight o'clock June nights . . . the dead
    men and the unborn children speak to me . . .
    I cannot tell you what they say . . . you listen
    and you know.

I don't care who you are, man:
I know a woman is looking for you,
and her soul is a corn-tassel kissing a south-west wind.

Haze

(The farm-boy whose face is the colour of brick-dust,
    is calling the cows; he will form the letter X with
    crossed streams of milk from the teats; he will beat
    a tattoo on the bottom of a tin pail with X's of
    milk.)

I don't care who you are, man:
I know sons and daughters looking for you,
And they are grey dust working toward star paths
And you see them from a garret window when you
    laugh
At your luck and murmur, 'I don't care.'

I don't care who you are, woman:
I know a man is looking for you,
And his soul is a south-west wind kissing a corn-tassel.

(The kitchen girl on the farm is throwing oats to the
    chickens and the buff of their feathers says hello
    to the sunset's late maroon.)

I don't care who you are, woman:
I know sons and daughters looking for you
And they are next year's wheat or the year after hidden
    in the dark and loam.

My love is a yellow-hammer spinning circles in Ohio,
    Indiana. My love is a redbird shooting flights in
    straight lines in Kentucky and Tennessee. My love
    is an early robin flaming an ember of copper on

243

her shoulders in March and April. My love is a
greybird living in the eaves of a Michigan house
all winter. Why is my love always a crying thing
of wings?

On the Indiana dunes, in the Mississippi marshes, I
have asked: Is it only a fishbone on the beach?
Is it only a dog's jaw or a horse's skull whitening in
the sun? Is the red heart of man only ashes? Is the
flame of it all a white light switched off and the
power house wires cut?

Why do the prairie roses answer every summer? Why
do the changing repeating rains come back out of
the salt sea wind-blown? Why do the stars keep
their tracks? Why do the cradles of the sky rock
new babies?

151. Buffalo Dusk

THE buffaloes are gone.
  And those who saw the buffaloes are gone.
Those who saw the buffaloes by thousands and how
    they pawed the prairie sod into dust with their
    hoofs, their great heads down pawing on in a
    great pageant of dusk,
Those who saw the buffaloes are gone.
And the buffaloes are gone.

152. Branches

THE dancing girls here . . . after a long night of
   it . . .
The long beautiful night of the wind and rain in
   April,
The long night hanging down from the drooping
   branches of the top of a birch tree,
Swinging, swaying, to the wind for a partner, to the
   rain for a partner.
What is the humming, swishing thing they sing in
   the morning now?
The rain, the wind, the swishing whispers of the long
   slim curve so little and so dark on the western
   morning sky . . . these dancing girls here on
   an April early morning . . .
They have had a long cool beautiful night of it with
   their partners learning this year's song of April.

153. The Windy City

I

THE lean hands of wagon men
    put out pointing fingers here,
picked this crossway, put it on a map,
set up their sawbucks, fixed their shotguns,
found a hitching place for the pony express,
made a hitching place for the iron horse,
the one-eyed horse with the fire-spit head,
found a homelike spot and said, 'Make a home,'
saw this corner with a mesh of rails, shuttling
        people, shunting cars, shaping the junk of
        the earth to a new city.

The hands of men took hold and tugged
And the breaths of men went into the junk
And the junk stood up into skyscrapers and asked:
Who am I? Am I a city? And if I am what is my
        name?
And once while the time whistles blew and blew again
The men answered: Long ago we gave you a name,
Long ago we laughed and said: You? Your name is
        Chicago.
Early the red men gave a name to a river,
        the place of the skunk,
        the river of the wild onion smell,
        Shee-caw-go.

The Windy City

Out of the pay day songs of steam shovels,
Out of the wages of structural iron rivets,
The living lighted skyscrapers tell it now as a name,
Tell it across miles of sea-blue water, grey-blue land:
I am Chicago, I am a name given out by the breaths of
      working men, laughing men, a child, a belonging.

So between the Great Lakes,
The Grand De Tour, and the Grand Prairie,
The living lighted skyscrapers stand,
Spotting the blue dusk with checkers of yellow,
      streamers of smoke and silver,
         parallelograms of night-grey watchmen,
Singing a soft moaning song: I am a child, a belonging.

II

How should the wind songs of a windy city go?
Singing in a high wind the dirty chatter gets blown
      away on the wind—the clean shovel,
                  the clean pickaxe,
                  lasts.

It is easy for a child to get breakfast and pack off
      to school with a pair of roller skates,
         buns for lunch, and a geography.

248

The Windy City

Riding through a tunnel under a river running back-
    ward, to school to listen . . . how the Pottawat-
    tamies . . . and the Blackhawks . . . ran on
    moccasins . . . between Kaskaskia, Peoria, Kan-
    kakee, and Chicago.

It is easy to sit listening to a boy babbling
    of the Pottawattamie moccasins in Illinois,
    how now the roofs and smokestacks cover miles
    where the deerfoot left its writing
    and the foxpaw put its initials
    in the snow . . . for the early moccasins . . . to
        read.

It is easy for the respectable taxpayers to sit in the
    street cars and read the papers, faces of burglars,
    the prison escapes, the hunger strikes, the cost of
    living, the price of dying, the shop gate battles of
    strikers and strikebreakers, the strikers killing
    scabs and the police killing strikers—the strongest,
    the strongest, always the strongest.

It is easy to listen to the haberdasher customers hand
    each other their easy chatter—it is easy to die
    alive—to register a living thumb-print and be dead
    from the neck up.

The Windy City

And there are sidewalks polished with the footfalls of
   undertakers' stiffs, greased mannikins, wearing up-
   to-the-minute socks, lifting heels across doorsills,
   shoving their faces ahead of them—dead from the
   neck up—proud of their socks—their socks are the
   last word—dead from the neck up—it is easy.

III

Lash yourself to the bastion of a bridge
and listen while the black cataracts of people go by,
         baggage, bundles, balloons,
         listen while they jazz the classics:

         'Since when did you kiss yourself in
         And who do you think you are?
         Come across, kick in, loosen up.
         Where do you get that chatter?'

         'Beat up the short change artists.
         They never did nothin' for you.
         How do you get that way?
         Tell me and I'll tell the world.
         I'll say so, I'll say it is.'

         'You're trying to crab my act.
         You poor fish, you mackerel,
         You ain't got the sense God
         Gave an oyster—it's raining—
         What you want is an umbrella.'

The Windy City

'Hush baby—
I don't know a thing.
I don't know a thing.
　　Hush baby.'

'Hush baby,
It ain't how old you are,
It's how old you look.
It ain't what you got,
It's what you can get away with.'

'Bring home the bacon.
Put it over, shoot it across.
　Send 'em to the cleaners.
What we want is results, re-sults
　And damn the consequences.
　　Sh . . . sh. . . .
You can fix anything
If you got the right fixers.'

'Kid each other, you cheap skates.
Tell each other you're all to the mustard—
You're the gravy.'

'Tell 'em, honey.
Ain't it the truth, sweetheart?
　Watch your step.
　You said it.
　You said a mouthful.
We're all a lot of damn fourflushers.'

The Windy City

'Hush baby!
Shoot it,
Shoot it all!
Coo coo, coo coo'—
This is one song of Chicago.

IV

It is easy to come here a stranger and show the whole
works, write a book, fix it all up—it is easy to come
and go away a muddle-headed pig, a bum and a
bag of wind.

Go to it and remember this city fished from its
depths a text: 'Independent as a hog on ice.'
Venice is a dream of soft waters, Vienna and Bagdad
recollections of dark spears and wild turbans; Paris
is a thought in Monet grey on scabbards, fabrics,
façades; London is a fact in a fog filled with the
moaning of transatlantic whistles; Berlin sits amid
white scrubbed quadrangles and torn arithmetics
and testaments; Moscow brandishes a flag and re-
peats a dance figure of a man who walks like a
bear.
Chicago fished from its depths a text: Independent
as a hog on ice.

V

Forgive us if the monotonous houses go mile on mile
Along monotonous streets out to the prairies—

The Windy City

If the faces of the houses mumble hard words
At the streets—and the street voices only say:
'Dust and a bitter wind shall come.'
Forgive us if the lumber porches and doorsteps
Snarl at each other—
And the brick chimneys cough in a close-up of
Each other's faces—
And the ramshackle stairways watch each other
As thieves watch—
And dooryard lilacs near a malleable iron works
Long ago languished
In a short whispering purple.

And if the alley ash cans
Tell the garbage wagon drivers
The children play the alley is Heaven
And the streets of Heaven shine
With a grand dazzle of stones of gold
And there are no policemen in Heaven—
Let the rag-tags have it their way.

And if the geraniums
In the tin cans of the window sills
Ask questions not worth answering—
And if a boy and a girl hunt the sun
With a sieve for sifting smoke—
Let it pass—let the answer be—
'Dust and a bitter wind shall come.'

The Windy City

Forgive us if the jazz timebeats
Of these clumsy mass shadows
Moan in saxophone undertones,
And the footsteps of the jungle,
The fang cry, the rip claw hiss,
The sneak-up and the still watch,
The slant of the slit eyes waiting—
If these bother respectable people
    with the right crimp in their napkins
    reading breakfast menu cards—
    forgive us—let it pass—let be.

If cripples sit on their stumps
And joke with the newsies bawling,
'Many lives lost! many lives lost!
Ter-ri-ble ac-ci-dent! many lives lost!'—
If again twelve men let a woman go,
'He done me wrong; I shot him'—
Or the blood of a child's head
Spatters on the hub of a motor truck—
Or a 44-gat cracks and lets the skylights
Into one more bank messenger—
Or if boys steal coal in a railroad yard
And run with humped gunnysacks
While a bull picks off one of the kids
And the kid wriggles with an ear in cinders,
And a mother comes to carry home
A bundle, a limp bundle,

The Windy City

To have his face washed, for the last time,
Forgive us if it happens—and happens again—
And happens again.

Forgive the jazz timebeat
of clumsy mass shadows,
footsteps of the jungle,
the fang cry, the rip claw hiss,
the slant of the slit eyes waiting.

Forgive us if we work so hard
And the muscles bunch clumsy on us
And we never know why we work so hard—
If the big houses with little families
And the little houses with big families
Sneer at each other's bars of misunderstanding;
Pity us when we shackle and kill each other
And believe at first we understand
And later say we wonder why.

Take home the monotonous patter
Of the elevated railroad guard in the rush hours:
'Watch your step. Watch your step. Watch your step.'
Or write on a pocket pad what a pauper said
To a patch of purple asters at a whitewashed wall:
'Let every man be his own Jesus—that's enough.'

The Windy City

VI

The wheelbarrows grin, the shovels and the mortar
    hoist an exploit.
The stone shanks of the Monadnock, the Transporta-
    tion, the People's Gas Building, stand up and
    scrape at the sky.
The wheelbarrows sing, the bevels and the blue prints
    whisper.

The library building named after Crerar, naked
    as a stock farm silo, light as a single eagle
    feather, stripped like an airplane propeller,
    takes a path up.
Two cool new rivets say, 'Maybe it is morning,'
    'God knows.'

Put the city up; tear the city down;
    put it up again; let us find a city.
Let us remember the little violet-eyed
    man who gave all, praying, 'Dig and
    dream, dream and hammer, till your
    city comes.'

Every day the people sleep and the city dies;
    every day the people shake loose, awake and
    build the city again.

The Windy City

The city is a tool chest opened every day,
    a time clock punched every morning,
    a shop door, bunkers and overalls
    counting every day.

The city is a balloon and a bubble plaything
    shot to the sky every evening, whistled in
    a ragtime jig down the sunset.

The city is made, forgotten, and made again,
    trucks hauling it away haul it back
    steered by drivers whistling ragtime
    against the sunsets.
Every day the people get up and carry the city,
    carry the bunkers and balloons of the city,
    lift it and put it down.

    'I will die as many times
    as you make me over again,
    says the city to the people,
'I am the woman, the home, the family,
I get breakfast and pay the rent;
I telephone the doctor, the milkman, the undertaker;
    I fix the streets
    for your first and your last ride—
'Come clean with me, come clean or dirty,

The Windy City

I am stone and steel of your sleeping numbers;
    I remember all you forget.
    I will die as many times
    as you make me over again.'

Under the foundations,
Over the roofs,
The bevels and the blue prints talk it over.
The wind of the lake shore waits and wanders.
The heave of the shore wind hunches the sand piles.
The winkers of the morning stars count out cities
And forget the numbers.

VII

At the white clock-tower
lighted in night purples
over the boulevard link bridge
only the blind get by without acknowledgments.
The passers-by, factory punch-clock numbers,
    hotel girls out for the air, teameoes,
        coal passers, taxi drivers, window washers,
        paperhangers, floorwalkers, bill collectors,
        burglar alarm salesmen, massage students,
        manicure girls, chiropodists, bath rubbers,
        booze runners, hat cleaners, armhole basters,
        delicatessen clerks, shovel stiffs, work plugs—

The Windy City

They all pass over the bridge, they all look up
    at the white clock-tower
    lighted in night purples
    over the boulevard link bridge—
And sometimes one says, 'Well, we hand it to 'em.'

Mention proud things, catalogue them.
The jack-knife bridge opening, the ore boats,
    the wheat barges passing through.
Three overland trains arriving the same hour,
    one from Memphis and the cotton belt,
    one from Omaha and the corn belt,
    one from Duluth, the lumberjack and the iron
    range.
Mention a carload of shorthorns taken off the valleys of
    Wyoming last week, arriving yesterday, knocked
    in the head, stripped, quartered, hung in ice boxes
    to-day, mention the daily melodrama of this hum-
    drum, rhythms of heads, hides, heels, hoofs hung
    up.

VIII

It is wisdom to think the people are the city.
It is wisdom to think the city would fall to pieces
    and die and be dust in the wind
If the people of the city all move away and leave no
    people at all to watch and keep the city.
It is wisdom to think no city stood here at all until the
    working men, the laughing men, came.

The Windy City

It is wisdom to think to-morrow new working men, new
     laughing men, may come and put up a new city—
Living lighted skyscrapers and a night lingo of lanterns
     testify to-morrow shall have its own say-so.

IX

Night gathers itself into a ball of dark yarn.
Night loosens the ball and it spreads.
The lookouts from the shores of Lake Michigan
     find night follows day, and ping! ping! across
     sheet grey the boat lights put their signals.
Night lets the dark yarn unravel, Night speaks and the
     yarns change to fog and blue strands.

The lookouts turn to the city.
The canyons swarm with red sand lights
     of the sunset,
The atoms drop and sift, blues cross over,
     yellows plunge.
Mixed light shafts stack their bayonets,
     pledge with crossed handles.
So, when the canyons swarm, it is then the
     lookouts speak
Of the high spots over a street . . . mountain language
Of skyscrapers in dusk, the Railway Exchange,
The People's Gas, the Monadnock, the Transportation,
Gone to the gloaming.
The river turns in a half circle.

The Windy City

The Goose Island bridges curve
    over the river curve.
    Then the river panorama
    performs for the bridge,
    dots . . . lights . . . dots . . . lights,
    sixes and sevens of dots and lights,
    a lingo of lanterns and searchlights,
    circling sprays of grey and yellow.

x

A man came as a witness saying:
'I listened to the Great Lakes
And I listened to the Grand Prairie,
And they had little to say to each other,
A whisper or so in a thousand years.
"Some of the cities are big," said one.
"And some not so big," said another.
"And sometimes the cities are all gone,"
Said a black knob bluff to a light green sea.'

Winds of the Windy City, come out of the prairie,
    all the way from Medicine Hat.
Come out of the inland sea blue water, come where they
    nickname a city for you.

Corn wind in the fall, come off the black lands,
    come off the whisper of the silk hangers,
    the lap of the flat spear leaves.

261

The Windy City

Blue water wind in summer, come off the blue miles
    of lake, carry your inland sea blue fingers,
    carry us cool, carry your blue to our homes.

White spring winds, come off the bag wool clouds,
    come off the running melted snow, come white
    as the arms of snow-born children.

Grey fighting winter winds, come along on the tearing
    blizzard tails, the snouts of the hungry
    hunting storms, come fighting grey in winter.

Winds of the Windy City,
Winds of corn and sea blue,
Spring wind white and fighting winter grey,
Come home here—they nickname a city for you.

The wind of the lake shore waits and wanders.
The heave of the shore wind hunches the sand piles.
The winkers of the morning stars count out cities
And forget the numbers.

154. Upstream

THE strong men keep coming on
    They go down shot, hanged, sick,
        broken.
They live on fighting, singing,
        lucky as plungers.
The strong mothers pulling them
        on . . .
The strong mothers pulling them
        from a dark sea, a great prairie,
        a long mountain.
Call hallelujah, call amen, call
        deep thanks.
The strong men keep coming on.

155. Four Steichen Prints

THE earth, the rock and the oil of the earth, the slippery frozen places of the earth, these are for homes of rainbow bubbles, curves of the circles of a bubble, curves of the arcs of the rainbow prisms— between sun and rock they lift to the sun their foam feather and go.

. .

Throw your neck back, throw it back till the neck muscles shine at the sun, till the falling hair at the scalp is a black cry, till limbs and knee bones form an altar, and a girl's torso over the fire-rock torso shouts hi yi, hi yee, hallelujah.

. .

Goat girl caught in the brambles, deerfoot or fox-head ankles and hair of feeders of the wind, let all the covering burn, let all stopping a naked plunger from plunging naked, let it all burn in this wind fire, let the fire have it in a fast crunch and a flash.

. .

They threw you into a pot of thorns with a wreath in your hair and bunches of grapes over your head—your hard little buttocks in the thorns—then the black eyes, the white teeth, the nameless muscular flair of you, rippled and twisted in sliding rising scales of laughter; the earth never had a gladder friend; pigs, goats, deer, tawny tough-haired jaguars might understand you.

156. Moon Riders

I

WHAT have I saved out of a morning?
  The earliest of the morning came with moon-mist
And the travel of a moon-spilt purple;
    Bars, horseshoes, Texas longhorns,
    Linked in night silver,
    Linked under leaves in moonlit silver,
    Linked in rags and patches
    Out of the ice houses of the morning moon.
    Yes, this was the earliest—
    Before the cowpunchers on the eastern rims
    Began riding into the sun,
    Riding the roan mustangs of morning,
    Roping the mavericks after the latest stars.
    What have I saved out of a morning?
    Was there a child face I saw once
    Smiling up a stairway of the morning moon?

II

'It is time for work,' said a man in the morning.
He opened the faces of the clocks, saw their works,
Saw the wheels oiled and fitted, running smooth.
'It is time to begin a day's work,' he said again,
Watching a bullfinch hop on the rain-worn boards
Of a beaten fence counting its bitter winters.
The slinging feet of the bullfinch and the flash

Moon Riders

Of its flying feathers as it flipped away
Took his eyes away from the clocks, his flying eyes.
He walked over, stood in front of the clocks again
And said, 'I'm sorry; I apologize forty ways.'

III

The morning paper lay bundled
Like a spear in a museum
Across the broken sleeping room
Of a moon-sheet spider.
The spinning work of the morning spider's feet
Left off where the morning paper's pages lay
In the shine of the web in the summer dew grass.
The man opened the morning paper, saw the first page,
The back page, the inside pages, the editorials,
Saw the world go by, eating, stealing, fighting,
Saw the headlines, date lines, funnies, ads,
The marching movies of the workmen going to work,
    the workmen striking,
The workmen asking jobs—five million pairs of eyes
    look for a boss and say, 'Take *me*,'
People eating with too much to eat, people eating with
    nothing in sight to eat to-morrow, eating as though
    eating belongs where people belong.

'Hustle, you hustlers, while the hustling's good,'
Said the man, turning the morning paper's pages,
Turning among headlines, date lines, funnies, ads.
'Hustlers carrying the banner,' said the man

Moon Riders

Dropping the paper and beginning to hunt the city,
Hunting the alleys, boulevards, back-door by-ways,
Hunting till he found a blind horse dying alone,
Telling the horse, 'Two legs or four legs—it's all the
    same with a work plug.'

    A hayfield mist of evening saw him
    Watching moon riders lose the moon
    For new shooting stars—he asked,
'Christ, what have I saved out of a morning?'
He called up a stairway of the morning moon
And he remembered a child face smiling up that same
    stairway.

157. At the Gates of Tombs

CIVILIZATIONS are set up and knocked down
the same as pins in a bowling alley.

Civilizations get into the garbage wagons
and are hauled away the same as potato
peelings or any pot scrapings.

Civilizations, all the work of the artists,
inventors, dreamers of work and genius,
go to the dumps one by one.

Be silent about it; since at the gates of tombs
silence is a gift, be silent; since at the epitaphs
written in the air, since at the swan songs hung in
the air, silence is a gift, be silent; forget it.

If any fool, babbler, gabby mouth, stand up and say:
Let us make a civilization where the sacred and
beautiful things of toil and genius shall last

If any such noisy gazook stands up and makes himself
heard—put him out—tie a can on him—lock him up
in Leavenworth—shackle him in the Atlanta hoose-
gow—let him eat from the tin dishes at Sing Sing—
slue him in as a lifer at San Quentin.
It is the law; as a civilization dies and goes down

At the Gates of Tombs

to eat ashes along with all other dead civilizations
—it is the law all dirty wild dreamers die first—
gag 'em, lock 'em up, get 'em bumped off.

And since at the gates of tombs silence is a gift,
be silent about it, yes, be silent—forget it.

158. Hazardous Occupations

JUGGLERS keep six bottles in the air.
Club swingers toss up six and eight.
The knife throwers miss each other's
        ears by a hair and the steel quivers
        in the target wood.
The trapeze battlers do a back-and-forth
        high in the air with a girl's feet
        and ankles upside down.
So they earn a living—till they miss
        once, twice, even three times.
So they live on hate and love as gipsies
        live in satin skins and shiny eyes.
In their graves do the elbows jostle once
        in a blue moon—and wriggle to throw
        a kiss answering a dreamed-of applause?
Do the bones repeat: It's a *good* act—
        we got a *good* hand. . . .?

159. Crossing the Paces

THE Sioux sat around their wigwam fires
in winter with some papooses hung up
and some laid down.
And the Sioux had a saying, 'Love grows
like hair on a black bear's skin.'

The Arabians spill this: The first grey
hair is a challenge of death.
A Polish blacksmith: A good black-
smith is not afraid of smoke.
And a Scandinavian warns: The world was born
in fire and he who is fire himself will be
at home anywhere on earth.
So a stranger told his children: You are
strangers—and warned them:

Bob your hair; or let it grow long;
Be a company, a party, a picnic;
Be alone, a nut, a potato, an orange blossom,
      a keg of nails; if you get lost try a
      want ad; if night comes try a long sleep.

160.   Harsk, Harsk

I

HARSK, harsk, the wind blows to-night.
What a night for a baby to come into the world!
What a night for a melodrama baby to come
        And the father wondering
        And the mother wondering
What the years will bring on their stork feet
Till a year when this very baby might be saying
On some storm night when a melodrama baby is born:
        'What a night
        for a baby
        to come into the world!!'
Harsk, harsk, the wind blows to-night.

II

It is five months off.
Knit, stitch, and hemstitch.
Sheets, bags, towels, these are the offerings.
When he is older—or she is a big girl—
There may be flowers or ribbons or money
For birthday offerings. Now, however,
We must remember it is a naked stranger
Coming to us, and the sheath of the arrival
Is so soft we must be ready, and soft too.
Knit, stitch, hemstitch, it is only five months.

Harsk, Harsk

III

It would be easy to pick a lucky star for this baby
If a choice of two stars lay before our eyes,
One a pearl gold star and one pearl silver,
And the offer of a chance to pick a lucky star.

IV

When the high hour comes
Let there be a light flurry of snow,
A little zigzag of white spots
    Against the grey roofs.
The snow-born all understand this as a luck-wish.

161. Brancusi

BRANCUSI is a galoot; he saves tickets to take him nowhere; a galoot with his baggage ready and no time table; ah yes, Brancusi is a galoot; he understands birds and skulls so well, he knows the hang of the hair of the coils and plaits on a woman's head, he knows them so far back he knows where they came from and where they are going; he is fathoming down for the secrets of the first and the oldest makers of shapes.

Let us speak with loose mouths to-day not at all about Brancusi because he has hardly started nor is hardly able to say the name of the place he wants to go when he has time and is ready to start; O Brancusi, keeping hardwood planks around your doorsteps in the sun waiting for the hardwood to be harder for your hard hands to handle, you Brancusi with your chisels and hammers, birds going to cones, skulls going to eggs— how the hope hugs your heart you will find one cone, one egg, so hard when the earth turns mist there among the last to go will be a cone, an egg.

Brancusi you will not put a want ad in the papers telling God it will be to His advantage to come around and see you; you will not grow gabby and spill God earfuls of prayers; you will not get fresh and familiar

Brancusi

as if God is a next-door neighbour and you have counted
His shirts on a clothes line; you will go stammering,
stuttering and mumbling or you will be silent as a mouse
in a church garret when the pipe organ is pouring ocean
waves on the sunlit rocks of ocean shores; if God is
saving a corner for any battling bag of bones, there will
be one for you, there will be one for you, Brancusi.

162. The Rakeoff and the Getaway

'SHALL we come back?' the gamblers asked.
'If you want to, if you feel that way,' the answer.

And they must have wanted to,
they must have felt that way;
for they came back,
hats pulled down over their eyes
as though the rain or the policemen
or the shadows of a sneaking scar-face Nemesis
followed their tracks and hunted them down.

'What was the clean-up? Let's see the rakeoff,'
somebody asked them, looking into their eyes
far under the pulled-down hat rims;
and their eyes had only the laugh of the rain in them,
lights of escape from a sneaking scar-face Nemesis
hunting their tracks, hunting them down.

Anvils, pincers, mosquitoes, anguish, raspberries,
steaks and gravy, remorse, ragtime, slang,
a woman's looking-glass to be held in the hand
for looking at the face and the face make-up,
blackwing birds fitted on to slits
of the sunsets they were flying into,
bitter green waters, clear running waters,

The Rakeoff and the Getaway

standing pools ringing the changes
of all the triangles of the equinoxes of the sky,
        and a woman's slipper
        with a tarnished buckle,
        a tarnished Chinese silver buckle.

The gamblers snatched their hats off babbling,
'Some layout—take your pick, kid.'

And their eyes had yet in them
the laugh of the rain
and the lights of their getaway
from a sneaking scar-face Nemesis.

163. Two Humpties

THEY tried to hand it to us on a platter,
   Us hit in the eyes with marconigrams from moon
      dancers—
And the bubble busted, went flooey, on a thumb touch.

   So this time again, Humpty,
We cork our laughs behind solemn phizzogs,
Sweep the floor with the rim of our hats
And say good-a-bye and good-a-bye, just like that.

      To-morrow maybe they will be hit
      In the eyes with marconigrams
      From moon dancers.
Good-a-bye, our hats and all of us say good-a-bye.

164. This—For the Moon—Yes?

THIS is a good book? Yes?
Throw it at the moon.
Stand on the ball of your right foot
And come to the lunge of a centre fielder
Straddling in a throw for the home plate,
Let her go—spang—this book for the moon
—yes?
And then—other books, good books, even the
best books—shoot 'em with a long twist
at the moon—yes?

165. Slabs of the Sunburnt West

I

INTO the night, into the blanket of night,
Into the night rain gods, the night luck gods,
Overland goes the overland passenger train.

Stand up, sandstone slabs of red,
Tell the overland passengers who burnt you.

Tell 'em how the jacks and screws loosened you.
Tell 'em who shook you by the heels and stood you
    on your heads,
Who put the slow pink of sunset mist on your faces.

Panels of the cold grey open night,
Gates of the Great American Desert,
    Skies keeping the prayers of the wagon men,
    The riders with picks, shovels and guns,
On the old trail, the Santa Fé trail, the Raton pass
Panels, skies, gates, listen to-night while we send up
    our prayers on the Santa Fé trail.

    (A colossal bastard frog
    squats in stone.
    Once he squawked.
    Then he was frozen and
    shut up for ever.)

Slabs of the Sunburnt West

Into the night the overland passenger train,
Slabs of sandstone red sink to the sunset red,
Blankets of night cover 'em up.
Night rain gods, night luck gods, are looking on.

March on, processions.
Tie your hat to the saddle and ride, O Rider.
Let your ponies drag their navels in the sand.
Go hungry; leave your bones in the desert sand.
When the desert takes you the wind is clean.
The winds say so on a noisy night.

> The fingerbone of a man
> lay next to the handle of a frying pan
> and the footbone of a horse.

'Clean, we are clean,' the winds whimper on a noisy
night.

Into the night the overland passenger train,
And the engineer with an eye for signal lights,
And the porters making up berths for passengers,
And the boys in the diner locking the ice-box—
And six men with cigars in the buffet car mention 'civi-
lization,' 'history,' 'God.'

Into the blanket of night goes the overland train,
Into the black of the night the processions march,
> The ghost of a pony goes by,
> A hat tied to the saddle,
> The wagon tongue of a prairie schooner

Slabs of the Sunburnt West

And the handle of a Forty-niner's pickaxe
Do a shiver dance in the desert dust,
In the coyote grey of the alkali dust.
And—six men with cigars in the buffet car mention
  'civilization,' 'history,' 'God.'

Sleep, O wonderful hungry people.
Take a shut-eye, take a long old snooze,
    and be good to yourselves;
Into the night the overland passenger train
And the sleepers cleared for a morning sun
    and the Grand Canyon of Arizona.

II

A bluejay blue
and a grey mouse grey
ran up the canyon walls.

A rider came to the rim
Of a slash and a gap of desert dirt—
A long-legged long-headed rider
On a blunt and a blurry jackass—
Riding and asking, 'How come? How come?'

And the long-legged long-headed rider said:
'Between two ears of a blurry jackass
I see ten miles of auburn, gold and purple—
I see doors open over door-sills
And always another door and a door-sill.

282

Slabs of the Sunburnt West

Cheat my eyes, fill me with the float
Of your dream, you auburn, gold, and purple.
Cheat me, blow me off my pins on to footless floors.
Let me put footsteps in an airpath.
Cheat me with footprints on auburn, gold, purple
Out to the last violet shimmer of the float
Of the dream—and I will come straddling a jackass,
Singing a song and letting out hallelujahs
To the door sill of the last footprint.'

And the man took a stub lead pencil
And made a long memo in shorthand
On the two blurry jackass ears:—

'God sits with long whiskers in the sky.'
I said it when I was a boy.
I said it because long-whiskered men
Put it in my head to say it.
      They lied . . . about you . . . God . . .
      They lied. . . .

The other side of the five doors
and door-sills put in my house—
how many hinges, panels, door-knobs,
how many locks and lintels,
put on the doors and door-sills
winding and wild between
the first and the last door-sill of all?

Slabs of the Sunburnt West

'Out of the footprints on ten miles
of auburn, gold and purple—an old song comes:
These bones shall rise again,
Yes, children, these bones shall rise.

'Yonder past my five doors
are fifty million doors, maybe,
stars with knobs and locks and lintels,
stars with riders of rockets,
stars with swimmers of fire.

'Cheat my eyes—and I come again—
straddling a jackass—singing a song—
letting out hallelujahs.

'If God is a proud and a cunning Bricklayer,
Or if God is a King in a white gold Heaven,
Or if God is a Boss and a Watchman always watching,
I come riding the old ride of the humiliation,
Straddling a jackass, singing a song,
Letting out hallelujahs.

'Before a ten mile float
of auburn, gold, and purple,
footprints on a sunset airpath haze,
    I ask:
How can I taste with my tongue a tongueless God?
How can I touch with my fingers a fingerless God?
How can I hear with my ears an earless God?

Slabs of the Sunburnt West

Or smell of a God gone noseless long ago?
Or look on a God who never needs eyes for looking?

'My head is under your foot, God.
My head is a pan of alkali dust
your foot kicked loose—your foot of air
with its steps on the sunset airpath haze.

    (A bluejay blue
    and a grey mouse grey
    ran up the canyon walls.)

'Sitting at the rim of the big gap
at the high lash of the frozen storm line,
I ask why I go on five crutches,
tongues, ears, nostrils—all cripples—
eyes and nose—both cripples—
I ask why these five cripples
limp and squint and gag with me,
why they say with the oldest frozen faces:
    Man is a poor stick and a sad squirt;
    if he is poor he can't dress up;
    if he dresses up he don't know any place to go.

'Away and away on some green moon
a blind blue horse eats white grass.
    And the blind blue horse knows more than I do
    because he saw more than I have seen
    and remembered it after he went blind.

285

Slabs of the Sunburnt West

'And away and away on some other green moon
is a sea-kept child who lacks a nose I got
and fingers like mine and all I have.
And yet the sea-kept child knows more than
I do and sings secrets alien to me as light
to a nosing mole underground.
I understand this child as a yellow-belly
catfish in China understands peach pickers
at sunrise in September in a Michigan orchard.

    'The power and lift of the sea
      and the flame of the old earth fires under,
I sift their meanings of sand in my fingers.
I send out five sleepwalkers to find out who I am,
    my name and number, where I came from,
    and where I am going.
They go out, look, listen, wonder, and shoot a fire-
    white rocket across the night sky; the shot and the
    flare of the rocket dies to a whisper; and the night
    is the same as it always was.
They come back, my five sleepwalkers; they have an
    answer for me, they say; they tell me: *Wait*—
    the password all of them heard when the fire-white
    rocket shot across the sky and died to a whisper,
    the password is: *Wait*.

'I sit with five binoculars, amplifiers, spectroscopes,
I sit looking through five windows, listening, tasting,
    smelling, touching.
I sit counting five million smoke fogs.

Slabs of the Sunburnt West

Repeaters, repeaters, come back to my window sills.
Some are pigeons coming to coo and coo and clean their
     tail feathers and look wise at me.
Some are pigeons coming with broken wings to die with
     pain in their eyes on my window sills.

'I walk the high lash of the frozen storm line;
I sit down with my feet in a ten-mile gravel pit.
Here I ask why I am a bag of sea-water fastened
to a frame of bones put walking on land—here I
look at crawlers, crimson, spiders spotted with
purple spots on their heads, flinging silver nets,
two, four, six, against the sun.
Here I look two miles down to the ditch of the sea
and pick a winding ribbon, a river eater, a water
grinder; it is a runner sent to run by a stop-watch,
it is a wrecker on a rush job.'

     (A bluejay blue
     and a grey mouse grey
     ran up the canyon walls.)

Battering rams, blind mules, mounted policemen,
trucks hauling caverns of granite, elephants
grappling gorillas in a death strangle, cathedrals,
arenas, platforms, somersaults of telescoped rail-
road train wrecks, exhausted egg heads, piles of
skulls, mountains of empty sockets, mummies of kings
and mobs, memories of work gangs and wrecking crews,

sobs of wind and water storms, all frozen and held
on paths leading on to spirals of new zigzags—

An arm-chair for a one-eyed giant;
two pine trees grow in the left arm of the chair;
a bluejay comes, sits, goes, comes again;
a bluejay shoots and twitters . . . out and across . . .
tumbled skyscrapers and wrecked battleships,
walls of crucifixions and wedding breakfasts;
ruin, ruin—a brute gnashed, dug, kept on—
kept on and quit: and this is It.
Falling away, the brute is working.
Sheets of white veils cross a woman's face
An eye socket glooms and wonders.
The brute hangs his head and drags on to the job.
The mother of mist and light and air murmurs: Wait.

The weavers of light weave best in red,
    better in blue.
The weavers of shadows weave at sunset;
    the young black-eyed women run, run, run
    to the night star homes; the old women
    sit weaving for the night rain gods,
    the night luck gods.

Eighteen old giants throw a red gold shadow ball;
they pass it along; hands go up and stop it; they
bat up flies and practise; they begin the game, they
knock it for home runs and two-baggers; the pitcher
put it across in an out- and an in-shoot drop; the

Slabs of the Sunburnt West

Devil is the Umpire; God is the Umpire; the game
is called on account of darkness.

> A bluejay blue
> and a grey mouse grey
> ran up the canyon walls.

III

Good night; it is scribbled on the panels
of the cold grey open desert.
Good night; on the big sky blanket over the
Santa Fé trail it is woven in the oldest
Indian blanket songs.

Buffers of land, breakers of sea, say it and
say it, over and over, good night, good night.

> Tie your hat to the saddle
> and ride, ride, ride, O Rider.
> Lay your rails and wires
> and ride, ride, ride, O Rider.

> The worn tired stars say
> you shall die early and die dirty.
> The clean cold stars say
> you shall die late and die clean.

> The runaway stars say
> you shall never die at all,
> never at all.